C000165151

Bluepr...

Studies on what the Bible has
to say about how we handle money,
wealth and possessions

Mark Lloydbottom

Foreword

The Bible has much to say about money, wealth and possessions, about God's generosity in his provision for us and our
need to exercise wise stewardship of this.

Spending time reflecting on God's Word reminds, challenges
and extends our thinking as we realise that as Christians, we
already have a blueprint for managing money and lifestyle. In
these forty reflections Mark Lloydbottom draws on a wealth of
scripture relating to debt, budgeting, lifestyle, giving and money
management. Oh, and a whole bunch of other topics as well!
For money touches every part of our lives – that's why it's such a
key topic for those of us who would count ourselves as followers
of Jesus. Paul teaches us that the love of money is a root of all
kinds of evil (1 Tim 6:10). Whilst we should not serve money, nor
place our trust in it, nor pursue what money can buy, this doesn't
mean that we should not think about it nor take the time and
effort to exercise wise stewardship over it.

I'm convinced that spending time with the Bible changes us,
and I commend these reflections to you, and encourage you to
set some time aside over the next forty days to read and pray
through them.

Dr John Preston
National Stewardship Officer, Church of England

With thanks

I want to express my sincere thanks to those who have assisted me in the writing of Blueprint. They include Rev. Osien Sibanda, who undertook some of the early research. I thank my wife, Rhoda, for her wisdom and enthusiasm. I am grateful to my editors and Gillian Searl. I value the willingness of Patricia Jones to provide encouragement and to write the daily prayer at the end of each devotional.

Special thanks is due to Edward Hobbs, former Director of Stewardship Ministries at First Baptist, Woodstock, GA, USA, who kindly allowed me to use resources from some of the ministry programs he has developed while counselling those in need of godly counsel.

I am grateful to the team at Compass, USA, who have sought faithfully to teach what the Bible says about our money and possessions. Some of the insights of Larry Burkett (1939-2003) and Howard Dayton, are also included.

Over the years I have been greatly enriched by reading some of the enduring hymns and words of saints who in many instances now live in heavenly places and I have taken the opportunity of sharing some of these inspiring words. I have even recorded some words of those who may not have known Jesus Christ as Lord and Saviour, but who expressed words of wisdom that are aligned with the Bible. It is a privilege to be the author of a book that includes the words of John Wesley,

Aiden Tozer, Billy Graham, Rick Warren, Oswald Chambers, Corrie Ten Boom, William Carey, Isaac Watts, John Maxwell, Ron Blue, Epictetus, Clive Staples Lewis and many others.

Mark Lloydbottom

Your Money Counts
www.yourmoneycounts.org.uk

Author's introduction

Our lives are interwoven with decisions about money and possessions. Those with enough have as many challenges as those who do not.

I was inspired to write Blueprint by Rhoda, my wife, who commits herself at the outset of each day to read her Oswald Chambers devotional. I thought that it would be valuable to record insights that provide both spiritual and, in the case of some days, practical steps about how to handle money and possessions.

Never before have there been so many opportunities to spend and the money we spend is often not ours – it is borrowed. For some, their wealth defines them. For Christians it is our faith that defines us although we recognise that we conform in so many ways to society's ways and means.

Each day's reading is accompanied by 'words of wisdom'. These are intended to be insights and reflections as you study each day.

I refer to the 2,350 verses that are in the Bible and refer throughout to what God says about how we are to handle our money and possessions. These studies include more than 300 of those Bible verses.

ABOUT MARK LLOYDBOTTOM AND YOUR MONEY COUNTS

Mark is the founder of Your Money Counts in the UK. Your Money Counts is affiliated with Compass, a ministry dedicated to sharing biblical financial principles around the world. Your Money Counts and all those associated with the Compass ministry seek to equip people worldwide to learn, apply and teach God's financial principles so they may know Christ more intimately, be free to serve Him and help fund the Great Commission.

Table
of
contents

PART 2

41 Free to serve Him

PART 3

93 Growing in generosity

PART 4

127 Save. Invest. Spend

PART 5

205 Just do it

"You were bought at a price; do not become slaves of men."

1 Corinthians 7:23

The Bible:
a blueprint
for living

Ownership | Stewardship | Provision

Ownership

How wonderful is our Father's Handbook

The Word of God well understood and religiously obeyed is the shortest route to spiritual perfection. And we must not select a few favourite passages to the exclusion of others. Nothing less than a whole Bible can make a whole Christian.

A W Tozer

I am profitably engaged in reading the Bible. Take all of this Book that you can by reason and the balance by faith, and you will live and die a better man. It is the best Book which God has given to man.

Abraham Lincoln

The Bible amazingly reveals God's plans. "In the beginning was the Word, and the Word was with God, and the Word was God...and the Word became flesh and made His dwelling among us" (John 1:1,14). Jesus the Word was there before the beginning and the role the members of the holy trinity played in Creation is made clear in Genesis. God's written Word is powerful today. It teaches us everything we need for life: "as His divine power has given to us all things that pertain to life and godliness" (2 Peter 1:3, NKJV) and indicates we can do good works to please Him (Ephesians 2:10). It even teaches us "how" to please him: for example in our social interactions, as employees, in marital and family relationships, and most importantly in the handling of money and possessions. The Living Word (Jesus Christ) gave us the written Word so that we will know how to live for Him.

How amazing to know God's only Son, Jesus, died that we might live forever. God's love is so great that He prepares a place for us in eternity. Our life on earth is so short although in younger years it does not appear to be so. The Bible reminds us that we may have a life span of just over 650,000 hours (seventy five years), yet He cares for us moment by moment and day by day.

YOUR DAILY STUDIES

These studies are not a replacement for your own Bible study. Blueprint seeks to illuminate the truth of the Bible and give us understanding when we allow the Holy Spirit to speak to our inner self through meditation and prayer – telling God what you want Him to know and listening to Him. Prayer is indeed a two-way process of speaking *to* God and listening *for* God. This devotional journey will focus on hearing God in your handling money and possessions.

Many view the Bible as hard to understand and sometimes unfathomable. If this is you, take heart, you are not alone. Many have never read the Bible from cover to cover and some who have may not fully comprehend all they read. The Bible is nearly impossible to fully understand much less obey without the enabling of the Holy Spirit.

THE ONLY BOOK GOD HAS WRITTEN

The Bible is the only book that God ever wrote. We should read the Bible understanding that it is our manufacturer's handbook. The Bible is where we look, just like an owner's manual for a household appliance, to find how to live, how to avoid problems, how to fix problems, how to succeed and how to live our lives according to His Word. Unlike other handbooks, however, the Bible needs no updates. Furthermore it does not start at the beginning or finish at the end with life on earth, for at the end of life on earth eternity is promised!

For the word of God is living and active. Sharper than any double-edged sword, it penetrates even to dividing soul and spirit, joints and marrow; it judges the thoughts and attitudes of the heart.

Hebrews 4:12

Blueprint is grounded in Scripture and godly wisdom. The Church in Thessalonica received the Word with readiness and searched the Scriptures to find out whether what the disciples taught was true (Acts 17:11). Since the Bible is our reference source let us look at its background – after all it is the book to which Christians turn to learn more about God, His ways, His plans, and His purposes.

I am a creature of a day. I am a spirit come from God, and returning to God. I want to know one thing: the way to heaven. God himself has condescended to teach me the way. He has written it down in a book. Oh, give me that book! At any price give me the book of God. Let me be a man of one book.

John Wesley

BIBLE FACTS

The word 'bible' means 'books.' There are 66 of them comprising 1,189 chapters – in the King James version that includes 31,102 verses and more than 775,000 words! The Bible was written over a period of 1,500 years – the oldest book is Job, whose authorship is unknown. There were more than 40 authors whose occupations were as diverse as kings, peasants, philosophers, tentmakers, shepherds, fishermen and scholars. It was written on three continents (Asia, Africa and

Europe) and in three languages (Hebrew, Aramaic and Greek). It includes more than 1,200 promises, almost 6,500 commands and over 8,000 predictions.

Although the Bible may have been penned by men the author is unquestionably God himself. It is *HIS*tory. In the middle chapter and verse (Psalm 118: 8) we read the Bible's central theme that it is, "better to trust in God than in man."

If you want to find out what God wants you to know about prayer or faith you have a resource of about 500 Bible verses for each. If you want to learn what God has to say about how we handle our money, wealth and possessions there are 700 direct verses referring to money and in total 2,350 verses referring to money, wealth and possessions. Fifteen per cent of Jesus' recorded words are about handling money and possessions. If you have listened to a preacher and thought that the Bible spoke mainly about giving (to the Church), be blessed, amazed and encouraged as you study these forty devotional readings. The sheer scale of what the Bible has to say demands our attention for it is clear that God knows the financial temptations that lie in this area. And His wisdom found in Scripture will help you avoid many financial pitfalls.

GOD'S FINANCIAL SYSTEM UNVEILED

In 2 Timothy 3:16 we read, "all Scripture is given by inspiration of God and is profitable for doctrine, reproof, for correction, for instruction in righteousness" (KJV). Note that

He chose to give us birth through the word of truth, that we might be a kind of firstfruits of all he created.

James 1:18

Take the helmet of salvation and the sword of the Spirit, which is the word of God.

Ephesians 6:17

the Bible says *all* Scripture and not some. Through faith we accept Jesus Christ as Saviour. If our salvation is only about eternity why would we not go direct to heaven instead of living here on earth? It is because our purpose on earth is to share our faith and live a life that pleases Him.

There is a close correlation between our true spiritual condition and how we handle our money and possessions. There are many areas where we may wonder how God wants us to handle our finances but we do not need to conjecture because the Bible is very clear in this area. God's biblical financial system differs from that of the world's – and one of the main differences is that God's economy works whereas the world's does not! God's economy says you are more blessed by giving than receiving. God promises much for our obedience, especially in financial matters as we shall explore during these devotional studies.

Thank you, Father, for speaking throughout the ages with love, hope and relevance to everyone in every era through your written word, the Bible. It is wonderful that you are interested in every aspect of my daily life including how I handle my finances. I want to learn and apply your financial principles in my life – give me a fresh hunger for your word, open my ears to hear and a willing heart to obey and change my ways to your Kingdom ways. In Jesus' name. Amen

God's part and our part

Gold is a symbol of value and a rare mineral. For centuries many cultures, including western countries, have regarded it as a safe investment. It is estimated that there are only five billion ounces of gold on this earth. How much is that? Imagine a 20-metre cube (you could have two such cubes in one half of a football pitch) – that is all the space you need to store all the gold in the world! Five billion ounces, much of it locked away stored in bank vaults. Who owns all this gold? Who is the true owner?

The world asks: "What does a person own?" God asks, "How is the person using what they have been given?" Your use of money shows what you think of God. We will be judged on the basis of our loyalty to Christ with the time, talents, and treasures that were at our disposal.

Erwin W. Lutzer, Pastor, Moody Church

GOD OWNS IT ALL

In 1 Chronicles 29:11-12 we read that, "everything in the heavens and earth is yours, O Lord and this is your Kingdom. We adore you as being in control of everything" (TLB). Psalm 24:1, Deuteronomy 10:14 and Paul in 1 Corinthians 10:26 all attest to the fact, "that the earth is the Lord's and everything in it." Leviticus 25:23 and Psalm 50:10-12 tell us just some of what God owns – "the land, the cattle, the birds," while Paul writes in 1 Corinthians 6:20, "we too have been bought for a price...therefore glorify God in your body, and in your spirit, which are God's" (NKJV). And Haggai 2:8 makes it clear

Everything in the heavens and on earth is yours, O Lord, and this is your Kingdom. We adore you as the one who is over all things. Wealth and honour come from you alone, for you rule over everything. Power and might are in your hand, and at your discretion people are made great and given strength.

1 Chronicles 29:11-12, NLT

that God owns all the gold. In Tutankhamen's day it was believed that when you died you could take your possessions with you, but the seventh verse and sixth chapter of the first letter of Timothy says, "it is certain we can carry nothing out" (1 Timothy 6:7, NKJV); Paul makes it clear no balances are transferred to us anywhere after we die.

RECOGNISING GOD'S OWNERSHIP

Our society and laws are based on ownership and responsibility – what you possess, you own. Acknowledging God's ownership requires a transformation of the way we think – and that takes time as the revelation from God's Word sends spiritual pulses from the brain to the heart. Recognising God's ownership is an essential component of becoming content. When you believe you own a particular possession, the circumstances surrounding it will affect your attitude.

GOD IS OUR PROVIDER

As Matthew states, the Lord promises to provide our needs: "Seek first his Kingdom and his righteousness, and all these things will be given to you as well" (6:33). To what extent does He provide? He promises to meet our needs for the necessities of life such as food, clothing and shelter. Our wants are desires that exceed our needs.

OUR PART

Recognising that we are stewards means that we must manage what He owns. God has given us the responsibility of being stewards, "you made him ruler over the works of your hands; you put everything under his feet" (Psalm 8:6). We are called to be faithful stewards with all that we are given, as illustrated by the parable of the talents in Matthew 25:14-15. God requires us to be faithful with all our money, wealth and possessions.

BEING FAITHFUL

In the parable of the unjust manager (Luke 16:1-2) we read, "There was a rich man whose manager [steward] was accused of wasting his possessions. So he called him in and asked, 'What is this I hear about you? Give an account of your management, because you cannot be manager [steward] any longer.'"

This passage teaches two principles. First, when we waste or mismanage our possessions it could become public knowledge and create a poor testimony. Second, God may remove us as stewards if we squander what He has given to us.

As we are faithful in little things, then God knows He can trust us with greater responsibilities. Small things are small things, but faithfulness with a small thing is a big thing.

DEVELOPMENT OF CHARACTER

God uses money to refine our character. As David McConaughy explained in his book, Money the Acid Test (written in 1918), "Money, most common of temporal things, involves uncommon and eternal

This book of the law shall not depart out of thy mouth; but thou shalt meditate therein day and night, that thou mayest observe to do according to all that is written therein: for then thou shalt make thy way prosperous, and then thou shalt have good success

Joshua 1:8, KJV

Now to him who is able to do immeasurably more than all we ask or imagine, according to his power that is at work within us.

Ephesians 3:20

consequences. Even though it may be done quite unconsciously, money moulds people in the process of getting it, saving it, spending it, and giving it. Depending on how it's used, it proves to be a blessing or a curse. Either the person becomes master of the money, or the money becomes the master of the person. Our Lord uses money to test our lives and as an instrument to mould us into the likeness of himself."

"Everything in the heavens and earth is yours, O Lord and this is your Kingdom. We adore you as being in control of everything"! Everything! That means, my home, my clothes, my car, my money. How tightly I hold these things as mine! Forgive my presumption, Father God – they are yours and come from your loving hand alone. Forgive all the times I have wasted your provision and been careless and selfish with your Kingdom property.

I prise each finger off everything – it all belongs to you. Thank you for this revelation – keep renewing my thinking in this vital truth so my practical actions will follow in line as a faithful steward – grow my character in this, you are in control now. Amen

Principles and promises

Scriptural principles have been tested over time and for many generations. They can be trusted, they are dependable and they work for those who live their lives accordingly. What a blessing to know God is in control and He has good plans for us. Paul tells us all Scripture has come from God in order to teach us, guide us, correct us and instruct us in righteousness. In this case righteousness refers to both our character and our actions. Basing our lives on Scripture reshapes our value systems, which in turn determines how we make or earn our living, how we spend what we earn and even how we save money.

He who has God and everything has no more than he who has God alone.

C S Lewis

BUILDING OUR LIVES ON GOD'S WORD

It is imperative therefore to make certain our value systems are built on God's Word, which gives a firm foundation. When it comes to a person's real nature, money plays a major role – for some it is even the primary role. How we handle money indicates an exact index to our godly character. Throughout Scripture, there is an intimate relationship between the development of character and how money is handled. There

The vigour of our spiritual lives will be in exact proportion to the place held by the Bible in our lives and in our thoughts.

George Müeller

is a powerful correlation between our true spiritual condition and our attitudes toward handling our money and possessions.

When Zacchaeus encountered the instruction of the living word in the form of Jesus Christ, his value system was transformed! Instead of taking and stealing from people, he gave back more than he had taken. He no longer focussed on himself but on what Scripture teaches: the interests of others. Zacchaeus was transformed. Instead of stealing and focusing on himself, he understood the concept of living well with others. It was the instruction from Jesus that transformed his behaviour. Jesus summed up this change in Zacchaeus as a Kingdom experience. Living in obedience to God and living rightly with his neighbours followed his understanding and acceptance of God's Word.

Jesus said, "today salvation has come to this house," (Luke 19:9) not because Zacchaeus prayed, but because he encountered a revelation with the Scriptures in living form and understood the right way to live with others. He in obedience, gave to the poor and ceased to trust in uncertain riches. He understood that Scripture instructs, "watch out and be on guard against all greed, because one's life is not in the abundance of his possessions" (Luke 12:15). These principles recur throughout Scripture. No wonder Jesus spoke more about money and possessions than any other single subject in the Bible. He wanted our value system to be aligned with His ways and not those of the world.

Where riches hold dominion of the heart, God has lost His authority.

John Calvin

WE WILL ALL GIVE AN ACCOUNT

One of the teachings of Scripture is that not only believers but everybody will give an account of their lives to the Lord. What are you doing to ensure when that day comes, you will be able to give a good account of yourself? Having accepted Jesus as Saviour is your journey through life drawing you closer to the Creator? Look at your attitude toward money – it provides a litmus test as to whether you have surrendered all to Him.

The lust for affluence in contemporary society has become psychotic: it has completely lost touch with reality.

Richard Foster

WE ARE TO BE OBEDIENT

It is important to know that God does not require us to be poor. The Bible has over 300 passages about the poor and social justice. We will look at what the Bible has to say concerning the poor later. There is a promise that depends on obedience to God's word or instructions and commands. Verse one of Deuteronomy 28 lays the condition, "if you fully obey...." Scripture promises us rewards for obeying God's instructions.

God's promises are always dependent on obedience to His commands. This clearly shows that the Lord has a particular course for us to follow but that He wants to guide us through. For us to stay on course with Him, He gives promises to keep us focussed. His promises are there to encourage us to trust and depend on Him. In Psalm 23 David observes "The Lord is my shepherd...He leads me..." God is ultimately in control of virtually everything we do and He has a purpose for all of us. If we stay focussed and believe His promises, we will be blessed.

GOD'S PROMISES

God's promises embrace every aspect of
our lives, from our work, children, families,
possessions through to eternal life. One
of God's promises is that He allows us to
prosper. He also says if we lose anything for
His sake we will find it. The promise here is
that whatever we give to someone in need
it is seen by God as an investment in His
Kingdom. His promises lead us to His ways,
which in turn direct us to His paths that lead
to His presence, where He is.

*Where God guides, He provides. What God
orders, he pays for. God's work, done in God's
way, never lacks God's supply.*

When we find Him, we are blessed because
He also promises that we will find Him when
we seek Him if we seek Him with all our
heart. We rid ourselves of worldliness when
we encounter the Heavenly. 'Thy Kingdom
come and thy will be done on earth as it is in
Heaven' was Jesus' prayer. His will is to be a
God who provides and leads us to well being.
We must believe the promises of God to
receive the benefits from them. Our obedience
to His commands allows the promises to
continue blessing us. This has been compared
to a brick and mortar building. Believing
the promises are the bricks and obeying the

commands is the mortar. You need both brick
and mortar: belief and obedience.

SCRIPTURAL PRINCIPLES

Scriptural principles have been tested
through time and for many generations.
They can be trusted, they are dependable
and they work for those who live their lives
accordingly. What a blessing to know God is
in control and that He has good plans for us.

It is important to make certain that our
value systems are built on God's Word, which
gives our lives a firm foundation. When it
comes to a man's real nature, money plays a
major role – for some it is even the primary role.

*In a world where ideas and value systems are constantly
shifting I thank and praise you, Father, that you are
eternal and that your word is eternal and true – a solid
safe foundation that cannot be shifted. Your word alone
is life changing and I choose to build my life on your
salvation and value system. Thank you for the clarity in
the accounts of the lives of those you had dealings with
in the Bible. My heart's desire is to be able to give a good
account of my life, in your presence. Forgive me when I
take for granted what you have given me to use for the
benefit of your Kingdom – help me turn around, away
from greed and selfishness to practice generosity and
selflessness with 'my' possessions. Amen*

"The earth is the Lord's, and everything in it, the world, and all who live in it."

Psalm 24:1

Stewardship

The character of stewardship

The earth is the Lord's, and everything in it, the world, and all who live in it.

Psalm 24:1

The story is told of a man who went to John Wesley to report that his house was on fire. "Mr. Wesley...your house has burned to the ground," he said, to which Wesley replied, "No. The Lord's house burned to the ground. That means one less responsibility for me." John Wesley understood the principle of stewardship – we are privileged to be stewards of what God owns, and He owns all things.

'Steward' can be defined as: Someone entrusted with another's wealth or property and charged with the responsibility of managing it in the owner's best interest – not ours.

Job understood the principle well. After he lost his family and property he understood that he did not own anything and refused to blame or curse God. Understanding stewardship alleviates stress and allows God to take charge.

WE ARE MANAGERS

Stewardship recognises that, "God owns everything and I am His manager/steward." Almost every book in the Bible refers to the Genesis account of creation. He created everything and what He asks of us is to live without allowing wealth or possessions to become the focus of our attention. He is a jealous God and He knows us from the beginning to the end of our days. He knows our weaknesses and frailties, and He knows that unless we submit what we have to Him we will not have an eternal perspective. He wants us to be good managers until we go to be with Him or the Lord's return – whichever comes first.

Some may find the subject of stewardship particularly difficult in two main areas: children, wealth and possessions. The earth is the Lord's and everything in it and even those who dwell in it. Understanding true ownership is an important element in managing what we have. It helps us to obey the Word when instructed to give and help the poor or destitute. It becomes a privilege to help the needy around us as we see God's provision not only for ourselves but also for others.

God delegates to us the authority over His Creation and commands us to manage and look after it all (Genesis 1:28). This refers not just to animals, ourselves, our family or our possessions but to everything over which we have influence. God requires us to be responsible and good managers of whatever He has given us, and in this respect we are working for God. There is a judgement coming and we are required to use God's resources wisely.

A faithful man will be richly blessed, but one eager to get rich will not go unpunished.

Proverbs 28:20

WE ARE TO BE FAITHFUL AND ACCOUNTABLE

Two characteristics stand out when we recognise this perspective of stewardship. The first is the faithfulness to the owner and

The heaven, even the heavens, are the Lord's: but the earth hath he given to the children of men.

Psalm 115:16, KJV

the second is accountability because the owner can come at anytime and do some stocktaking. In the parable of the talents (Matthew 25:14-30) we learn that a servant is required to be faithful. We must be faithful with what God entrusts to us. He promised that He would reward us for using his assets wisely. The more we have, the more assiduous we should be in using wisely what the master has put in our hands. Stewards are not to be lazy; they should be wise, seeking opportunities for growth and increase. The master is coming and he will deal with us according to how we have used our talents, possessions, influence and our lives. This parable teaches us that all those who are unproductive will lose what they are given.

Stewardship is what we do after we say 'I believe.'

The steward's life is to please and obey the master's instructions – and the Bible is replete with principles, instructions and wisdom. A wise steward uses what has been entrusted to them for God's glory and the building of His Kingdom. Unwise stewards use people and possessions selfishly.

THE SHREWD MANAGER

The story of the shrewd manager in Luke 16:1-9 demonstrates that what we do with what we've been given determines what we receive.

Your bank and credit card are theological.
They tell you who and what you worship.

Jesus told his disciples: "There was a rich man whose manager was accused of wasting his possessions. So he called him in and asked him, 'What is this I hear about you? Give an account of your management, because you cannot be manager any longer.'" The manager said to himself, 'What shall I do now? My master is taking away my job. I'm not strong enough to dig, and I'm ashamed to beg – I know what I'll do so that, when I lose my job here, people will welcome me into their houses.' So he called in each one of his master's debtors. He asked the first, 'How much do you owe my master?' 'Eight hundred gallons of olive oil,' he replied. "The manager told him, 'Take your bill, sit down quickly, and make it four hundred.'" Then he asked the second, 'And how much do you owe?' 'A thousand bushels of wheat,' he replied. "He told him, 'Take your bill and make it eight hundred.'"

The master commended the dishonest manager because he had acted shrewdly. "For the people of this world are more shrewd in dealing with their own kind than are the people of the light. I tell you, use worldly wealth to gain friends for yourselves, so that when it is gone, you will be welcomed into eternal dwellings."

Stewardship is the acceptance from God of personal responsibility for all of life and life's affairs.

Roswell C Long

HOW MUCH CAN GOD TRUST YOU WITH?

Whoever can be trusted with very little can also be trusted with much, and whoever is dishonest with very little will also be dishonest with much. So if you have not been trustworthy in handling worldly wealth, who will trust you with true riches? And if you have not been trustworthy with someone else's property, who will give you property of your own? No servant can serve two masters. Either he will hate the one and love the other, or he will be devoted to the one and despise the other. "You cannot serve both God and money. The Pharisees, who loved money, heard all this and were sneering at Jesus. He said to them, 'You are the ones who justify yourselves in the eyes of men, but God knows your hearts. What is highly valued among men is detestable in God's sight.'" Luke 16:10-15

You are asking me to be a faithful, accountable steward over those things you have entrusted to me. You, Father God, are my 'boss', your word is your manual and your Holy Spirit is my counsellor – I want to be a good steward and also to improve and grow in character and practice. Instruct me further in your Kingdom ways – I don't want to be lazy or lose what you have entrusted – I want to learn from you to be obedient and experience your blessings – and hear from you 'well done, my good and faithful servant' at the end of my days – when we meet face to face in eternity. Amen

DAY 05

Stewardship and contentment

If a portrait of a godly steward were to be drawn on canvas it would invariably show a very gracious and cheerful giver. Yet the words 'stewardship' and 'steward' seem to have less relevance today. To some it is just a religious cliché used to make fund-raising spiritual. It conjures up large red thermometers outside churches measuring how far we are from raising restoration funds.

God is not counting our giving for He judges the heart because He wants to be *our* treasure. Matthew 6:21 says, "for where your treasure is, there your heart will be also." God views us through the lens of our heart and, in one respect, our heart is the thermometer that represents our gracious giving. The act of gracious giving is a vivid reminder that our life is all about God and not about us, for the money that God entrusts us with has a higher purpose than our affluence. Gracious giving dethrones me and affirms Christ's Lordship. A gracious giver understands God when he says that we cannot serve both God and money. Giving breaks the chains of materialism that enslave people and places importance and emphasis on the 'heavenly places.'

If a person gets his attitude toward money straight, it will help straighten out almost every other area of his life.

Billy Graham

All the believers were together and had everything in common. Selling their possessions and goods, they gave to anyone as he had need. Every day they met together in the temple courts. They broke bread in their homes and ate together with glad and sincere hearts, praising God and enjoying the favour of all the people. And the Lord added to their number daily those who were being saved.

Acts 2:44-47

Jesus Christ said more about money than any other single thing because, when it comes to a man's real nature, money is of first importance. Money is an exact index to a man's true character. All through Scripture there is an intimate correlation between the development of a man's character and how he handles money.

Richard Halverson

GRACIOUS GIVING

Jesus taught us what He thought about gracious giving when He said, "Leave her alone... Why are you bothering her?" (Mark 14:6) about the woman who had anointed Him with oil. She had just given graciously and yet those around her considered her giving to be wasteful. Jesus said, "She has done a beautiful thing to me." What from an earthly perspective was a waste to some people in this woman's mind was a grateful and gracious – 'the best I could do' – action. Some thought this was fanatical giving but Jesus just called it 'LOVE'. In fact this was such an example of gracious giving that Jesus said, "Wherever the gospel is preached throughout the world, what she has done will also be told in memory of her" (Matthew 26:13). But gracious and generous giving is not a 'one size fits all' philosophy; Jesus also spoke of a poor widow who was able to give only two small coins. Yet compared to the rich who gave out of their abundance, Jesus said she gave more than they did. Our hearts will determine our gratitude to Jesus who gave Himself for us. Gracious giving is indeed the mark of a godly steward.

Moreover it is required in stewards that one be found faithful.

1 Corinthians 4:2, NKJV

IS GOD ENOUGH TO KEEP YOU CONTENT?

Contentment in life is as important as love, mercy or even fidelity. To be discontented is like saying to God, "you are not sufficient and you don't satisfy me." Contentment is not only a result of trusting God; it is also the means by which we trust God. Every day we are bombarded by the world's enticement to be dissatisfied with what we have. Enough is never enough! Paul tells Timothy to "keep the main thing the main thing" and that joy everlasting comes with contentment. "But godliness with contentment is great gain. For we brought nothing into this world, and we can take nothing out of it" (1 Timothy 6: 6-7). In Hebrews we read that we are advised to, "keep our lives free from the love of money and be content with what we have because God has said, 'Never will I leave you; never will I forsake you'" (Hebrews 13:5). While one of the wisdom books tells us, "Whoever loves money never has money enough...[and] is never satisfied with his income" (Ecclesiastes 5:10).

Money is a terrible master but an excellent servant.

P T Barnum

The Bible teaches that we should help fellow Christians in need and also show hospitality to strangers. Thus, every member of any local Church should be able to look to the fellowship they attend as an extension of God's provision.

Larry Burkett, Co-Founder Crown Financial Ministries, 1939–2003

HOW DEEP ARE YOUR ROOTS?

It has been said that money is like a spice in the smorgasbord of sinful desires. Most of us do not lust after money itself but rather the things money can obtain for us. Money gives us false security, comfort, approval

His master replied, 'Well done, good and faithful servant! You have been faithful with a few things; I will put you in charge of many things. Come and share your master's happiness.

Matthew 25:21

and power. It gets us what we want – and therein lies the root of many different kinds of evil. Money is our standard and method of exchange. The more we have, the more exchanges can occur, which enables the idolatry of money to take hold in our lives. Our heart turns from Christ to the things of this world when our roots are as shallow as money. Jesus even called the serving of money unrighteousness – and that should be a warning sign. This unrighteous obstacle can be so dangerous that it can keep a person from allowing Jesus to be Lord.

How perceptive and piercing are your words Lord, you know me through and through! We all love things and you love to bless us – but it is my heart attitude that endangers my walk with you. I turn away now from the unrighteous idolatry of money – forgive me, Lord God, dig that evil root out of me. I want to be like the lady who gave her precious oil to Jesus in worship and the poor widow who gave all she had for your Kingdom.
Again I recognise that all I have is yours. I am content – Thank You. Amen

Provision

What is our attitude toward our treasures?

Christians cannot experience peace in the area of their finances until they have surrendered total control of this area to God and accepted their position as stewards.

Larry Burkett

Don't waste your God-given life with low living, small planning, mundane talking, constant grumbling, or cheap giving. Be all God called you and equipped you to be.

What captivates your mind? What do you think about? What do you treasure? What do you spend doing longer than you perhaps ought to? What do you spend your money on?

Shopping has become a national obsession – the traffic queue outside our Church heading for the shopping centre at one o'clock on a Sunday afternoon suggests that the traditional family Sunday lunch is not the national appointment it used to be.

How many hours do you spend each week looking at a screen, whether a TV, game machine, mobile phone or a computer? Whatever the heart pursues dominion will ensue. If we pursue fleshly pursuits we will care less for the things of the Spirit but if we pursue the things of the Spirit we will concern ourselves less with the flesh. But ever since the fall of man in the Garden of Eden there has been an ongoing battle between flesh and spirit. Where the pursuit of riches holds dominion in the heart, God has lost His authority within.

WHERE IS YOUR TREASURE?

Matthew tells us, "for where your treasure is, there your heart will be also" (6:21, NKJV).

Here Jesus is telling us that our heart (desires, hopes, wants) is closely tied to our treasure. In fact, your heart often follows your money. If Jesus alerts us to this powerful tug of our heart it must be something we should pay close attention to. If you want to find out where your treasure is then examine your bank and credit card statements and you will see which side of this tug-of-war is winning. Your priorities will be evident from these statements. The spending of your income indicates where your heart is.

Yet indeed I also count all things loss for the excellence of the knowledge of Christ Jesus my Lord, for whom I have suffered the loss of all things, and count them as rubbish, that I may gain Christ.

Philippians 3:8, NKJ

WHAT'S YOUR ATTITUDE?

C. S Lewis once said, "He who has God and everything has no more than he who has God." The word 'everything' is a big word when it applies to mankind, but it diminishes greatly when mankind applies it to God.

There is a powerful correlation between a person's true spiritual condition and his or her attitude and actions concerning money and possessions. Jesus linked money and salvation together in Luke when Zacchaeus said he would give money back to the poor and pay back four times over to anyone he had cheated. Contrast that with the rich young ruler who had kept God's commandments but when he asked Jesus how he might inherit eternal life. Jesus replied, "Go sell your possessions and give to the poor, then come, follow me" (Matthew 19:21). Jesus knew that wealth owned this man rather than the other way round. He said it was easier for a camel to get down on its belly and try to crawl through a very small

Where God guides He provides. What God orders, He pays for. God's work, done in God's ways, never lacks supply.

opening than it was for a rich man to give up all his riches and enter the Kingdom of God. That same challenge is just as impossible today as it was when Jesus spoke these words.

What do we value most? What would we most hate to lose? What do our thoughts turn to most frequently when we are free to think of what we will? And finally, what affords us the greatest pleasure?

A W Tozer

A TEST OF CHARACTER

It has been said that how we handle money is a litmus test of our true character. It is also an index of our true spirituality.

If you are on the escalator to heaven you should not be conformed to the ways of this world – no matter how hard the path. The reality is that conformity is as natural as swimming downstream. Have you ever tried to swim against the current? It is hard and sometimes you even lose ground.

Where does a person go to get proper instruction? Well, books, magazines and the Internet are filled with advice and various plans on how to make, spend, save and invest money. How blessed we are to have the Bible from where we learn the perfect plan from the Lord Jesus Christ. Jeremiah 29:11 says, "I know the plans I have for you," declares

The world will never be won to Christ with what people can conveniently spare.

Bernard Edinger

the Lord; "plans to prosper you and not harm you, plans to give you hope and a future." Jesus said, "Store up for yourselves treasures in heaven, where moth and rust does not corrupt and thieves do not steal" (Matthew 6:20).

Martin Luther stated, *"each of us must have the conversion of the heart and mind and purse."* Let us assume that you have had the conversion of the heart. Now we must take on a new attitude by changing our minds to match that of Christ. If our mind is changed, God will again own all that is in the world – and He will have your purse. He already owns it but does it own us? We must allow Him to be Lord of our life and our treasures.

Naked a man comes from his mother's womb, and as he comes, so he departs. He takes nothing from his labour that he can carry in his hand.

Ecclesiastes 5:15

What wonderful words you spoke to Jeremiah those generations ago and still true today – 'I know the plans I have for you – plans to prosper you – 'me' – not harm me, plans to give me hope and a future'. Thank you for your plans even in the very details of my life – I want to change my mind so that I change my actions – search my heart and attitudes, especially those relating to money and possessions – 'treasure'. Show me where I have secret idols and the not so secret ones – strengthen my resolve to eradicate these from my life and worship you alone.
Amen

DAY
07

Giving materialism a wide berth

Blessed are they that hunger and thirst after righteousness: for they shall be filled.

Matthew 5:6, NKJV

It may help to give a definition of materialism: materialism is, 'having an undue regard for material and worldly things rather than spiritual matters. This is characterised by a preoccupation with material rather than intellectual or spiritual things.' So, based on this definition do you regard yourself as materialistic?

HOW MATERIALISTIC ARE YOU?

You might be materialistic if you spend money you do not have or buy goods you do not really need so as to indulge yourself or to impress others. Or maybe you compare the things you do not have with the possessions of others?

Ecclesiastes 5:10 tells us that, "Whoever loves money never has money enough..." Scripture tells us that if we look for love and fulfilment in our financial status we will never be satisfied. In the right context, material possessions can bring us joy, but when we attach greater importance to them than to things that should be more important, it harms our relationship with God and others. If we sacrifice our family or our relationship with God to have certain possessions, we are materialistic. Scripture enlightens us that a person who is greedy for more things is an idolater (Ephesians 5:5).

Some people want to make as much as they can, put the lid on the can and then sit on the can.

ONE MASTER ONLY?

In Matthew 6:24, Jesus tells us that we cannot serve two masters. When our passion for the possessions that God allows us to have exceeds our passion for the God who gave us those possessions, we know that we are materialistic. There is nothing wrong with owning things, the problem comes when those things get in the way of our relationship with God or prevent us from accomplishing God's will in our lives.

WHAT IS GREED?

Greed is the eager or selfish desire for something. When our desire for possessions consumes us and overtakes us to the point that we are not satisfied with what we have, it becomes greed. Luke 12:15 warns us to, "Watch out! Be on your guard against all kinds of greed; a man's life does not consist in the abundance of his possessions." Paul tells us to, "Put to death, therefore, whatever belongs to your earthly nature... and greed, which is idolatry" (Colossians 3:5). Greed may help us accumulate a lot of possessions but greed or possessions will not make us happy. Greed is also an offence against God and we should "put it to death."

Where riches hold the dominion of the heart, God has lost dominion of the heart, God has lost His authority.

John Calvin

Desires for a material possession usually fades once the newness wears off. Look in your garage, loft or storage room and see some of the things that you once thought were essential to life and happiness that are now not working, collecting dust, or simply adding to the general clutter. Look at the array of possessions that people seek to sell at car boot sales.

RICHES

Riches can be defined as an abundance of whatever is precious. Looked at in this perspective whether a person is rich or not depends on what we consider precious. What do you regard as precious?

All that truly matters is what we can do for the Kingdom of God. The things we accumulate are not important; they are only tools for us to use in accomplishing God's work. God owns it all anyway. The accumulation of money is a major deterrent to a humble spirit. The tendency is to desire to be served rather than to serve.

Larry Burkett, Co Founder, Crown Financial Ministries, 1939-2003

YOUR RELATIONSHIP WITH GOD

Paul says, "What is more, I consider everything a loss compared to the surpassing greatness of knowing Christ Jesus my Lord, for whose sake I have lost all things. I consider them rubbish, that I may gain Christ" (Philippians 3:7-8). Paul tapped into God's riches and realised that what the world had to offer was not even close to what God had given him. We have received a "precious faith" and "precious promises" in God's Word (2 Peter 1:1, 4).

Is your faith more precious than your possessions? Is living by His precious promises valuable to you?

YOUR FAMILY

We know that we are in trouble when our financial health becomes more important than our relationship with our family. We know that we have a wrong balance in life when we spend more hours working, watching TV or 'being on the computer' than spending time building family relationships and investing our lives in them.

We might think that if we work hard we can have more money to buy more possessions for our family, but in truth instead of having larger homes and newer cars, what they really want is for us to spend more time with them. Talk to someone who is retired and I am sure they will not say they wished they had spent more time working. No. They usually say, "I wish I had spent more time with my family or growing in my relationship with God."

ETERNAL RICHES

When Jesus was about to leave this earth and ascend to Heaven, he spoke the following words to his disciples, "In My Father's house are many mansions; if it were not so, I would have told you. I go to prepare a place for you. And if I go and prepare a place for you, I will come again and receive you to Myself; that where I am, there you may be also" (John

Then he [Jesus] said to them, "Watch out! Be on your guard against all kinds of greed; a man's life does not consist in the abundance of his possessions."

Luke 12:15

What good will it be for a man if he gains the whole world, yet forfeits his soul? Or what can a man give in exchange for his soul?

Matthew 16:26

14:2-3, NKJV). Jesus ascended into Heaven almost 2,000 years ago and since then He has been preparing a place for those who know Him as Lord and Saviour.

Forgive me Lord God when I have idolised things, cluttered up my life with them and worshipped that instead of You, pushing You out the way. Help me to turn away from materialistic choices of how I spend my time and money. I don't want to reach the end of my days and regret not spending time with You and my family – help me find the right balance and see what is really most precious – You and my family are waiting. Amen.

"Blessed are they that hunger and thirst after righteousness: for they shall be filled."

Matthew 5:6, NKJV

2

Free
to
serve
Him

Debt | The practical provision | Advice and counsel

Debt

DAY
08

The stranglehold of debt

No investment is as secure as a repaid debt.

Finnish Proverb

O money, money, money, I'm not necessarily one of those who thinks thee holy, but I often stop to wonder how thou canst go out so fast when thou comest in so slowly.

Ogden Nash, Poet, 1902 –1971

If there is one area of finance that tends to receive more attention than others it is the subject of debt. Personal debt and government debt. Many have succumbed to the temptation to spend now and think about repaying later.

The growth of personal debt is facilitated by access to credit via cards and loans while government debt arises when governments over commit their capital projects and welfare costs rise inexorably as people live longer.

Personal debt rose year on year after the Second World War until 2007. It was only the impact of the global financial crisis with loss of jobs and economic uncertainty that debt levels reduced. However when an economy grows it is evidenced that debt reverts to increasing.

Some types of personal debt incur interest charges that are far outside the realms of what many perceive normal and fair rates of interest. Payday loan companies may now be more closely monitored but they still charge rates that are what the Bible describes usury (excessive).

How serious is all of this? Very.

HOW HAS DEBT TAKEN SUCH A HOLD?

The first credit card was introduced in this country in 1966. Until that time households did not have computers and payments were normally made using cash or cheques. In the ensuing years, however, technology has advanced relentlessly while consumerism has gained a stranglehold in many households. There are now so many more goods to buy and so much more that people want (as distinct from need).

God's Word tells us that His plan for us is to be debt free. The blessings of becoming debt free go far beyond the financial area: they extend to the spiritual and marital realms. No one who is financially bound can be spiritually free.

Larry Burkett, Co Founder, Crown Financial Ministries, 1939–2003

Marketers tell us that we need something because, 'You're worth it,' and the Internet, cards, and PIN numbers facilitate the ready purchase of whatever we desire. With an economy that promotes easy access to credit and a materialist culture holding society in its grip, debt has become accepted and regarded as the norm. As a consequence, minds have become transformed and conformed to the ways of the world, leaving some people burying their heads in despair, overwhelmed by the problem of debt.

THE BIBLE ON DEBT

So what counsel can we find in the Bible concerning debt? Nowhere does the Bible command Christians not to assume debt, nor does Scripture say that debt is a sin, but the Bible does contain warnings about being in debt. Proverbs 22: 7 tells us that, "the borrower is slave [servant] to the lender." Our monetary system is largely based on debt; it seems so natural to be in debt, but is that not to some extent a result of people succumbing to the world's temptations? Paul in 1 Corinthians 7:23 reminds us that, "You were bought with a price; do not become slaves of men." The world's definition of debt is enjoying today those things that you cannot afford until tomorrow, in other words I want to enjoy instant gratification.

The Apostle Paul again commands us to, "present your bodies a living sacrifice, holy, acceptable to God, which is your reasonable service. And do not be conformed to this world, but be transformed by the renewing of your mind" (Romans 12:1-2, NKJV).

DEBT PRESUMES UPON TOMORROW

When we get into debt we assume that we will earn enough in the future to pay it off. Scripture cautions us against making presumptions: "Come now, you who say, 'Today or tomorrow, we will go to this or that city, spend a year there, carry on business and make money'. Why, you do not even know what will happen tomorrow.... Instead you ought to say 'If it is the Lord's will, we will live and do this or that'" (James 4: 12-15, NKJV).

DEBT MAY DENY GOD
AN OPPORTUNITY

The obvious alternative to borrowing in order to make purchases is to save until you can afford to pay for it. There is a sense in which saving and preparing to spend provides a restraining discipline by deferring the time when you will benefit from whatever it is you wish to acquire. In that time your desire to make that purchase may either evaporate or turn into a greater sense of ownership as you know that when you have finished saving you can buy and enjoy.

Say not my soul, "From whence
Can God relieve my care?"
Remember that Omnipotence
Has servants everywhere.
His method is sublime,
His heart profoundly kind;
God never is before His time,
And never is behind.

Thomas Toke Lynch,
English congregational minister, 1818-1871

On the other hand, there are those who have prayed and trusted God to provide. This provokes the question, does it require more faith to trust God to pay off our purchases made with debt or to wait on Him to provide before we make the purchase? It is important to understand that the Bible does not promise

You were bought at a price; do not become slaves of men.

1 Corinthians 7:23

that He will fulfil our carnal desires or provide the luxuries of this world (1 John 2:15-17) or riches, (1 Timothy 6:9-10) all of which can be snares.

Forgive me, Father God, for the times I have been discontent enough to enslave myself to debt. Where I am still enslaved show me how to reduce the debt and eventually be free from its stranglehold. As I see the dangers of debt and start to act to get free, I ask your blessing and strength as I rely on you and rest in you for your wisdom and provision. You have said 'not to be anxious about anything'. Thank you for showing me these financial principles and the way to financial freedom. Amen

When debt may be the way

It is always important to read Scripture in context – the Bible does not say that debt is a sin. God loves us so much that He gives us many guidelines and instructions so that we may be wise in our ways. He does not condemn us when we find ourselves in a mess. On the contrary, He sent Jesus specifically to reach out to those whose lives are in a mess. He gave us the Church as the body of Christ – not just a home for the redeemed, but a hospital for sinners!

How long will it take you to become debt free?

WHEN CAN WE BORROW?

The Bible is silent on when we can owe money. It warns against the dangers of debt, but does not preclude it. In my opinion it is possible to owe money for a home mortgage, to invest in a business, or to train for a career. However, we believe this is permissible only if the following four criteria are met:

1. The item purchased is an asset with the potential to appreciate or produce income

2. The value of an item equals or exceeds the amount owed against it

The wife of a man from the company of the prophets cried out to Elisha, "Your servant my husband is dead, and you know that he revered the Lord. But now his creditor is coming to take my two boys as his slaves."

2 Kings 4:1

3. The debt is not so high that repayment puts undue strain on your spending

4. The debt does not give rise to anxiety (Isaiah 32:17)

A home mortgage might meet the first requirement as, over time a house usually, but not always, appreciates. You can meet the second requirement by investing a reasonable deposit so that you would expect to sell the home for at least enough to repay the mortgage. The third requirement means buying an affordable house – one with a monthly repayment that does not strain your spending plan. Make sure you could continue to repay your mortgage even if the interest rates increased by two, or even three per cent and you have the necessary savings for unexpected cash requirements like repairs or maintenance.

God opposes usury and greed, yet no one realises this because it is not simple murder and robbery.

Martin Luther, Theologian, 1483 – 1546

How long should it take to repay? That is between you and God, make sure that if you move you do not extend the final date that you make that last mortgage payment. If you can, use relocation as an opportunity to bring forward that date by taking a mortgage with a shorter term than that remaining on the previous one.

A business owner may need to raise capital for the start or purchase of a business, or possibly to provide a source of working capital.

STUDENT DEBT

While students may receive some financial assistance from parents there is no doubt

Consolidation loans are tempting because you are able to pay off your creditors with the loan and then make one payment instead of several. However you are likely to pay more interest in the long term and more than 50 per cent of those who consolidate their loans increase their debts with the 'spare' cash. Thus these loans only treat the "symptoms" for a while but not the problem.

Larry Burkett, Co Founder, Crown Financial Ministries, 1939-2003

that student debt is a problem, with many people not completing their repayments until they are in their forties. These days, student debt is almost inevitable for those pursuing a degree, and although in some ways it is unique (you are unlikely to secure any other kind of loan at such a low rate of interest *or* with the repayments so directly linked to earnings) nevertheless it is still a burden of debt on people at the start of their adult lives. There is also a danger that it might lead to a sense that debt cannot be avoided with a consequential culture of debt that focuses on stretching to borrow the maximum that is affordable. Excessive student debt may limit your freedom of jobs you can take and in serving and ministering as God directs.

Make it your intention today to reduce your debt.

Just as the rich rule the poor, so the borrower is servant to the lender.

Proverbs 22:7, TLB

DO YOU HAVE A FINANCIAL ROADMAP?

We should not be like the Israelites who wandered in the wilderness for forty years on a journey that could have been done in 11 days (Deuteronomy 1:2) but rather we need to have a financial road map that will ensure that we do not suffer the burden of debt for one day longer than is absolutely necessary. This is important as in some cases debt repayment may require many extra years even beyond retirement.

WHEN DEBT HAS BEEN THE WAY

When should you not use debt? Resist the endeavours and strains of the companies who seek to tempt you with free credit – 'Buy today, pay tomorrow, only £x per month.' These and many similar offerings are the world's endeavours to snare you in debt.

Motor vehicles are often purchased using some form of debt finance. Here is an approach to breaking that cycle of debt. When you have finished paying for your car resist the temptation to replace it, rather continue saving your monthly repayments and then when you have been doing this for two or three years you will be able to replace the car using the value of your car and the accumulated savings. You may not even have to use all you have set aside!

Father God, thank you for your provision in my life, but as I look over my financial life today I realise there are financial decisions that I have taken, that with hindsight, could have been wiser. Show me any areas that you wish me to alter to come in line with your Kingdom ways. Give me the humility and wisdom to acknowledge where I have made mistakes or sinned and with Your help, and wise counsel, to change things. Thank you for caring so much about my life and how I live it for You. Amen

Tough times don't last

Money issues are a common component of 'tough times.' At the very least, the lack of money, or even of money and possessions themselves, often feature in these situations. Having too much can give rise to sleepless nights trying to protect, manage or grow what you have, whereas having too little can result in losing sleep trying to balance the budget and respond to the red demand letters. Having 'nothing' or being in debt makes people feel destitute and often a burden on family or the government. Proverbs puts it like this: "...give me neither poverty nor riches, but give me only my daily bread. Otherwise, I may have too much and disown you and say, 'Who is the Lord?' Or I may become poor and steal, and so dishonour the name of my God" (Proverbs 30:8-9).

Whatever the cause, if you cannot do what you want, when you want and where you want, frustration or anxiety arises, and this is often a precursor to stress, which can be debilitating and develop into illness, either physical, mental or both. Thus, those journeying through 'tough times' can experience seemingly insurmountable pain and this is a major factor in the distress and helplessness experienced. People respond in

Consider it pure joy, my brothers, whenever you face trials of many kinds, because you know that the testing of your faith develops perseverance.

James 1: 2-3

different ways – some seek a quick fix while others might be in denial, burying their heads in the sand unable to address the situation.

SEEKING GOD'S SOLUTION

The most common response is a quick fix or an early exit from the problem. This leaves open the possibility that the root issue is not fully addressed or that not all the lessons are learned. Then there is a danger that the problem will repeat itself when the abyss of 'tough times' once again opens up ahead of the weakness reappearing or recurring.

The Bible teaches us to stand with our focus on God. Paul tells us to, 'put on the whole armour of God,' (Ephesians 6:11, 13, NKJV). We are reminded twice to put on the whole armour because we are prone to not using it all because the whole armour may restrict our movement more than we desire. Matthew 6:33 instructs us to, "seek first his Kingdom and his righteousness." Do not succumb, but allow his Word to help you overcome the enemy of debt or the giant of overwhelming debt. Prayerfully seek God's counsel. However long it takes, keep praying ceaselessly until the Lord God answers. It could be that the 'tough times' are a result of an unexpected event, such as an unexpected car or household expense, the death of a loved one, or they may be the culmination of years of wrong living or neglect. These are faith-testing times and opportunities to reach out and find God in your situation – and be assured He is there even before you.

Difficulties are God's errands; and when we are sent them we should esteem it a proof of God's confidence – as a compliment from God.

Henry Ward Beecher, Clergyman, 1813-1887

Tough times don't last, but people do.

His oath, His covenant, His blood,
Support me in the raging flood;
When every earthly prop gives way,
He still is all my strength and stay.

Edward Mote, Hymn writer and English pastor, 1797 – 1874

THE TIMES WILL SURELY PASS

Declare in both your head and your heart that the situation is not permanent. It will surely pass, so what you do and how you respond is important. Patience is a shock absorber at such times. Do not be quick to make a decision. It is always best to avoid making decisions in the eye of a storm if you can. Hindsight often clarifies that a hasty action or decision was not the right course of action. The disciples were in fear when in the dark of the night they thought the storm held danger. Jesus reassured them and spoke calm into their minds.

You may sleep on an empty stomach but you will not die! People have been known to live without food for weeks, while others have managed without electricity for most of their lives. As surely as spring follows winter, it is a season and it too will pass. Learn the lessons of the seasons so that you can help others when they face similar circumstances and determine, so far as you are able to, not to walk through a time such as this again – or if

Character cannot be developed in ease and quiet. Only through experience of trial and suffering can the soul be strengthened, vision cleared, ambition inspired and success achieved.

Helen Keller,
1880 – 1968

you do, to know with godly assurance how to overcome what crosses your life's path.

The lowest ebb is the turn of the tide for there has never been a sunset yet, not followed by a sunrise.

LESSONS TO BE LEARNED

Tough times have many lessons to teach, and in most cases we desperately need those lessons. The author, broadcaster and missionary Elisabeth Elliot alludes to this in her statement, *"I am not a theologian or a scholar but I am very aware of the fact that pain is necessary to all of us, and tough times carry with them a great degree of pain. Out of the deepest pain comes the strongest conviction of the presence and the love of God."*

Allow God to speak to you clearly and hear the still small voice of calm that reassures you of His love. He speaks through His Word, the Bible, so look there *first* for answers. He once stood knocking at the door of your life waiting to be asked in. He *is still* with you and has given you the indwelling power and presence of his Holy Spirit; He is still waiting for you to invite Him into the situation you are in.

Through tests a Christian will learn to withstand tenaciously the pressure of a trial until God removes it at His appointed time and even cherish the benefit.

John MacArthur

Therefore put on the full armour of God, so that when the day of evil comes, you may be able to stand your ground, and after you have done everything, to stand.

Ephesians 6:13

The Psalmist says, "For You, O God, have tested us...you laid affliction on our backs. You have caused men to ride over our heads; we went through fire and through water; but You brought us out to rich fulfilment" (66:10,12, NKJV). There is a way out of every tough situation. It is easier when we focus on God – He is our loving heavenly Father who seeks to bless us and teach us. Job learned of God's love in the adversities he faced. Learn what God has to teach you and ensure you do not blame God for those 'tough time' situations.

Every humiliation, everything that tries and vexes us, is God's way of cutting a deeper channel in us through which the life of Christ can flow.

Oswald Chambers, Scottish Christian minister, 1874–1917

If we are quick to run to the bank manager, the credit card, our parents or aid agencies, we only lengthen our training period. For the children of Israel that meant forty years. But they came through in the end! Tough times are not a permanent phenomenon; they are temporary, so learn to see them as such.

How would you measure the amount of trust you have in God during tough times? Is it total, complete, unconditional, or is it limited by your view of your circumstances? God's Word says, "Trust in the Lord with all

The Lord is close to those whose hearts are breaking; He rescues those who are humbly sorry for their sins.

Psalm 34:18, TLB

your heart and do not lean on your own
understanding. In all your ways acknowledge
Him, and He will make your paths straight"
(Proverbs 3:5-6, NKJV).

Thank you Father, for your encouragement today –
thank you for the insights in your word that tell me I
am an overcomer; that you are with me through the
tough times and that you bring me through with 'songs
of deliverance' as I keep you as my 'hiding place'.
Thank you for every time you have answered prayer,
encouraged me, gone before me, brought me through,
rescued me, blessed me – I love you with all my heart
and soul, my saviour, friend, Lord and tester of my faith
– refine me in this season. Amen

"Trust in the Lord with all your heart and do not lean on your own understanding. In all your ways acknowledge Him, and He will make your paths straight."

Proverbs 3:5-6

The practical provision

Love and compassion

There is probably not a day in your life when you do not think about those you love. Equally, there is probably not a day when we do not hear or read about some act of hatred or vengeance.

Prince Charles once said to Diana, his wife to be, "I love you so much, whatever 'love' means." Love is a subject that has been written about extensively. The Greeks sought to classify it into three major forms: agape, phileo and eros.

Paul talks extensively about the importance of love in 1 Corinthians 13. Without it, he says, we are nothing but a clanging cymbal. He goes on to tell us that if we do not have love we have nothing (v 2) and that unless we act out of a heart of love we are nothing (v 3).

Love suffers long and is kind; it does not envy, it does not parade itself, it is not puffed up (v 4). Love does not behave rudely, does not seek its own, is not provoked, and thinks no evil (v 5). It does not rejoice in iniquity but in the truth (v 6). It bears all things, believes all things, hopes all things, and endures all things (v 7). Love never fails (v 8).

God proved His love on the cross. When Christ hung, and bled, and died, it was God saying to the world, "I love you."

Billy Graham

GOD'S GREAT LOVE

A true demonstration of love is seen in the Son of God on the streets of Jericho, Jerusalem, Judea, Samaria, right through to the cross on Calvary. He gave his life because He loved us and died that we might be reconciled to God and bridge the divide that our sin created between God and man. He does not ask us to endure what He endured, He does not require us to carry another cross and be crucified. God requires us only to accept His Son, love others and share the good news of Jesus and salvation and fulfil our role and responsibility in the Great Commission. It does not take wealth to practise these graces – we just have to have the love of God to allow compassion to flow.

The Scottish scientist and evangelist Henry Drummond (1851-1897) listed nine components of love: patience, kindness, generosity, humility, courtesy, unselfishness, good temper, lack of guile and sincerity. Love will always seek to do good or to make a positive difference. Love should cause us to want to be a blessing to others – to give of what we have. How can we claim to have the love of God if we fail to be part of alleviating the needs of those around us?

A new command I give you: Love one another. As I have loved you, so you must love one another. By this all men will know that you are my disciples, if you love one another.

John 13:34-35

LOVE IS THE GREATEST GIFT

There is good reason why Jesus told his disciples that love was the greatest gift as well as a commandment. O that we would sharpen and deepen the quality of our life through increasing these nine qualities. It would indeed make for a richer and more godly life. Is this possible? Of course, for these

Don't seek vengeance. Don't bear a grudge; but love your neighbour as yourself, for I am Jehovah.

Leviticus 19:18, TLB

Love cures people – both the ones who give it and the ones who receive it.

Carl Menniger,
1893-1990

ingredients flow from love – a gift from God.

Love acts as a conduit through which compassion flows. Love and compassion work in tandem. The Scriptures refer on numerous occasions to Jesus when He was moved with compassion toward people in need. That compassion was always followed by an act of love as Jesus sought to alleviate the suffering.

LOVE AND COMPASSION

As we live a life that is characterised by seeking to love others we should feel drawn to help practically. In 1 John 3:17 we read that "if anyone has material possessions and sees his brother in need but has no pity on him, how can the love of God be in him?" Compassion towards others is the consequence of unconditional love. Love is on the one hand a command and on the other, a choice. We are commanded to love by Scripture that we may be a channel of compassion.

Compassion is the instrument that puts us alongside our neighbours. It is the ability to sense the suffering the other person is feeling and to seek to help. Compassion literally means 'suffering with.'

If anyone has material possessions and sees his brother in need but has no pity on him, how can the love of God be in him.

1 John 3:17

Novelist, historian and human rights activist, Alexander Solzhenitsyn observed that mankind's sole salvation lies in everyone making everyone his business. Our western world today has families that are more separated and dysfunctional than ever before. Our society does not revolve around biblical standards, and our world does not function properly. The more we look at Jesus as our role model the more we will be drawn towards loving and helping others.

INVESTING GOD'S LOVE

We are to spread God's love not just abroad, but also at home with our family, friends and neighbours. As we go through life may our sensitivity to the need to love and help others increase. Investing in the lives of others is a privilege and an investment with a heavenly return.

Thank you, Father, for every person who has shown love and kindness to me – for that selfless love comes from You. You want us as your children to grow the fruit of love and practical compassion in our lives – help me to see the world through your eyes of love, and not walk by, unthinking, uncaring. I can care about the whole world in a sentimental way, but you have placed me in particular areas where I can show your love and compassion in practical ways. Open my eyes, my heart and my wallet to the needs of others – help me make Kingdom choices and become kind and generous with my time and money. Amen

Becoming debt free – part 1

Are you drowning in debt? Do you fear opening your post, or have you even stopped opening certain envelopes? Are you behind with your payments and receiving demands? Is your account being charged late payment fees? Is your expenditure greater than your income? Do you long for the day when your debts will be repaid and you will have peace of mind?

If any of these circumstances describes your situation it is time to rediscover your financial freedom. While you know that you are not alone, that is of little comfort as you recognise your part in getting into debt and acknowledge that you must now take action. Even if none of the above applies to you, you will almost certainly know someone who has debt, then pray for them as they work their way out of debt.

Today and tomorrow we seek to explore a biblical approach to becoming debt free by looking at twelve steps for getting out of debt.

Money talks...but all mine ever says is good-bye.

But before that can happen, you first need to make a decision that you will not incur one penny of additional debt; that building up of the debt mountain has to stop. Perhaps today is the day to make that decision. And once you have made it, prepare to start thinking about saving!

Now we will look at the first six of twelve steps to becoming debt free:

1. PRAY

In 2 Kings 4:1-7 we learn about the widow who was threatened with losing her children to her creditor and asked Elisha for help. Elisha instructed her to borrow many empty jars from her neighbours. The Lord then multiplied her only possession – a small amount of oil – and all her jars were filled. She then sold the oil and repaid her debts to free her children. The same God who provided supernaturally for the widow is interested in you becoming debt free. The first step is to pray and seek the Lord's help and guidance in your journey to become debt free. If you feel that you have borrowed beyond what was wise or necessary ask God to forgive you and to walk alongside you on the debt repayment journey.

For in the land the Lord your God is giving you to possess as your inheritance, he will richly bless you, if only you fully obey the Lord your God and are careful to follow all these commands I am giving you today. For the Lord your God will bless you as He has promised, and you will lend to many nations but will borrow from none. You will rule over many nations but none will rule over you.

Deuteronomy 15:4-6

2. STOP BORROWING

This is a step that can be extraordinarily difficult to take. It requires you to decide that you will not increase your borrowing. You need to decide it is time to stop letting your borrowing get any further out of control. Some have taken that step with the help of plastic surgery – cutting up their cards! Others have frozen their cards in ice so that it would take time to retrieve them! If you are concerned about how you will get along without your credit cards, rest assured you can train yourself to be independent of those 850x550mm pieces of plastic debt inducers!

3. RECORD YOUR EXPENDITURE

For the next month, record all your income and expenditure, down to the last penny – and note especially how you spend your cash. This requires discipline, but it is amazing how much more aware you will become of your spending habits and how sensitive you will become to reducing non-essential expenditure.

Credit and credit cards are not the problem; it is the misuse of credit that creates the problems. Four rules for using credit cards: never use them for anything other than budgeted purchases; pay them off every month; the first month you cannot pay the account, destroy the card and never use it again; keep in mind that just because you can afford something, you don't necessarily need it.

Larry Burkett

It usually takes time to get into debt. Increasing debt is like gaining weight – it results from indiscipline. Conversely, getting rid of debt is like shedding weight – it takes discipline! The excess debt pounds will be shed through more careful spending habits and diligently monitoring your expenditure. At the end of the month, total up your expenditure. Now you have some of the essential information for a needs-based (monthly or weekly) budget.

4. YOUR BUDGET WILL UNLOCK THE KEYS TO DEBT REDUCTION

Repayment of debts is a great investment.

Your daily devotional is not the right time to start preparing a budget, but it does provide an opportunity to examine your heart before God and to determine not to allow your future spending to be influenced so much by the world's materialistic paths. Remember that you are a steward of what you have been entrusted with. Ask yourself if and how you need to make changes to your spending patterns. How can you pare down your expenditure so that you can *invest* more in reducing your debt? As you meditate on these matters it is important to stay focussed on Christ and to trust in Him. Remember it took time to get into debt and it will probably take time to become debt free.

5. LIST WHAT YOU OWN

Evaluate your possessions to determine if there is anything you do not need that you could sell to help you get out of debt more quickly. What about the clothes you no longer wear or the technology you no longer use?

6. LIST WHAT YOU OWE

Many people do not know exactly what they owe, particularly if they owe a lot. Perhaps this is an aspect of human nature to avoid unpleasant things in the hope they will go away. In any event, you need to list your debts to determine your current financial position.

Wait on the Lord; be of good courage, and He shall strengthen your heart; wait, I say, on the Lord!

Psalm 27:14, NKJV

Tomorrow we will look at the final six steps to becoming debt free.

Father God, help me right now to be honest and accountable to you, myself and my family. I want to enjoy financial freedom and get rid of the weight of the anxiety of debt. I acknowledge and repent of the fact that I got myself into this mess. Help me to develop courage and patience as I work through and address the issues you have shown me. Thank you, for your love and presence – I need you and come as your child for a Fatherly embrace and for encouragement. Amen

Becoming debt free
– part 2

Paul informs the believers in the Church at Corinth that, "their bodies were bought at a price; do not become slaves of men" (1 Corinthians 7: 23). You will recall that Proverbs 22:7 reads, "Just as the rich rule the poor, so the borrower is servant to the lender" (TLB).

Why does the Lord not want us to become slaves to debt? Maybe it is because the debt and materialism in the 21st century competes with Him who we know is a jealous God. Maybe it is because the battles that we face are spiritual battles. When we are slaves to debt we are not as free to serve God or to fight the good fight. When our minds are fixed on the pleasures and technology of this world, they are not fixed on Him. When our lives are so committed to servicing debt we may find that Satan has us in a place where we are ineffective as ambassadors for Christ.

Again, Paul in his first letter to the Church at Corinth reminded believers that their bodies were a temple of the Holy Spirit, whom they had received from God. Paul wrote, "You were bought at a price. Therefore honour God with your body" (1 Corinthians 6:20). Let us recognise that getting out of debt is part of a battle that is not just being

> *A big part of being strong financially is that you know where you are weak and take action to make sure you don't fall prey to the weakness. And we all are weak.*
>
> **Dave Ramsey, US radio talk show host**

Neither a borrower not a lender be; for loan oft loses both itself and friend, and borrowing dulls the edge of husbandry.

Shakespeare, Hamlet

fought here on earth. Any debt mortgages the future as it presumes upon tomorrow and assumes that you will have the income to repay what is owed.

Continuing with the twelve steps on your path to freedom from debt:

7. ESTABLISH A DEBT REPAYMENT PLAN

There are a number of accepted approaches to repaying debt. One that is effective and popular is the 'debt snowball' approach.

With this approach, you list your debts with the smallest first and largest last. Then, you repay the minimum amount on all debts with the exception of the smallest, on which you repay as much as you can – and as quickly as possible. When it is repaid, roll the monthly/weekly amount you were repaying on that debt and add it to the amount you are paying off on the second debt. In this way your repayments will snowball from debt to debt.

8. CONSIDER EARNING ADDITIONAL INCOME

Many people hold jobs that simply do not pay enough to meet their needs, even if they spend wisely. If you are able to earn additional income, decide in advance to use it to pay off debts. Whether we earn much or little, we tend to spend more than we make, so be careful not to fall into the trap of spending the extra income. Remember that word of instruction from Ecclesiastes 5:10:

You are only poor when you want more than you have.

"whoever loves money never has money enough."

9. BE CONTENT WITH WHAT YOU HAVE

The advertising industry uses powerful methods to persuade people to buy. Frequently the message is intended to create discontent with what we have. Television, the Internet, and magazines all resonate with the message that we need to buy more 'stuff' – 'because you deserve it.'

In the consumer-driven economy:

The more adverts you look at the greater the temptation to spend. The more you look and admire what others have, the more you are likely to want to spend.

Christians who are trapped by borrowing have violated one or more of the scriptural principles God has given. He says that when someone borrows, he or she becomes a servant to the lender; the lender becomes an authority over the borrower. This clearly defines God's attitude about borrowing.

Larry Burkett

Paul informs the believers in the Church at Corinth that, "their bodies were bought at a price; do not become slaves of men" (1 Corinthians 7: 23). You will recall that

The wicked borrows and does not repay, but the righteous shows mercy and gives.

Psalm 37:21, NKJV

Proverbs 22:7 reads, "Just as the rich rule the poor, so the borrower is servant to the lender" (TLB).

Why does the Lord not want us to become slaves to debt? Maybe it is because the debt and materialism in the 21st century competes with Him who we know is a jealous God. Maybe it is because the battles that we face are spiritual battles. When we are slaves to debt we are not as free to serve God or to fight the good fight. When our minds are fixed on the pleasures and technology of this world, they are not fixed on Him. When our lives are so committed to servicing debt we may find that Satan has us in a place where we are ineffective as ambassadors for Christ.

Again, Paul in his first letter to the Church at Corinth reminded believers that their bodies were a temple of the Holy Spirit, whom they had received from God. Paul wrote, "You were bought at a price. Therefore honour God with your body" (1 Corinthians 6:20). Let us recognise that getting out of debt is part of a battle that is not just being fought here on earth.

The more you look at catalogues, magazines, door leaflets, Internet banner advertisements etc, the more you spend.

The more you shop, the more you spend.

It is probably something to do with the way we have all become wired because we are so accustomed to spending. Some even regard it as therapy! Paul writes, "But godliness with contentment is great gain" (1 Timothy 6:6). It is godly to be content and not always having something that we think we "must" buy. Someone who is addicted to drugs must have the next fix. In a similar way, our lack of contentment can be assuaged only by another dose of buying (even if we do not have the funds to actually spend).

10. CONSIDER A CHANGE IN LIFESTYLE

Some might decide they have to lower their standard of living to become debt free while others might sell a home and move to a smaller one, or even move to rented accommodation. As tough a decision as it might be, some people have transferred their children from private education to a state school. In short, they have temporarily sacrificed their standard of living or preferred options to be debt free in as short a time as possible. Then they achieve the financial freedom to really enjoy living again.

11. PRAY

I end where we started by encouraging you at all times to submit your finances to God. With over 2,300 verses – about seven and a half per cent of the Bible – referring to financial matters, there is much wisdom in God's Word and now that you have started on the road to getting out of debt I encourage you to continue the journey to biblical financial freedom. Spend much time in prayer, you will be given wisdom for your day including the ability to resist the temptation of debt or inappropriate spending. Jesus said, "Get up and pray so that you will not fall into temptation" (Luke 22:46). Prayer unlocks the power of God to work on our behalf.

Finally, be strong in the Lord and in his mighty power. Put on the full armour of God so that you can take your stand against the devil's schemes.

Ephesians 6:10–11

12. AND FINALLY –
LOVE FOR THE DAY IS NEAR

Paul charges the Church at Rome to, "Let no debt remain outstanding, except the continuing debt to love one another, for he who loves his fellowman has fulfilled the law" (Romans 13:8).

Lord God, I submit my finances to you and again ask for your help and wisdom in reaching financial freedom. At times the way can get tough – you have placed me in your family (your Church) and equipped the family with giftings and wisdom – there I can receive encouragement to stay on the path and complete the journey. Thank you for contentment and security that comes from You living in me and me living in You. You are an awesome God! Amen

DAY 14

Avoiding bankruptcy

Living on credit and not repaying what is owed is characteristic of the wicked. Psalm 37:21 says, "The wicked borrow and do not repay, but the righteous give generously." Christians should not behave in the same manner as 'the wicked.' Malachi records this, "I will be quick to testify against...those who defraud labourers of their wages" (Malachi 3:5) and this certainly also applies to those who have provided goods and services to us.

In bankruptcy, a court of law declares that a person is unable to pay his debts. Depending upon the type of bankruptcy, the court will either allow the debtor to develop a plan to repay his creditors or it will distribute his or her property among the creditors as payment for the debts. These modern bankruptcy procedures, including IVAs (Independent Voluntary Arrangements) provide a level of balanced legal protection for both the creditor and debtor. On the one hand, creditors have a fair entitlement to the debtor's assets if they have any. On the other, the law carries the benevolent intent of providing protection for the debtor with the objective that they can recover from the financial obligations and make a fresh start. Unfortunately, the system is subject to significant abuse and

Often all it takes to start down the road to bankruptcy is a small raise or increase in income.

Mark Lloydbottom

Is bankruptcy wrong? No, the law serves to protect the debtor and creditor.

Do all that you can to repay what is legitimally owed and gain victory over your debt.

is often manipulated for unjust ends. Our obligations as followers of Christ are to obey His commands to us and the principles understood here tell us to not defraud others or avoid paying those debts we incur.

SHOULD A CHRISTIAN DECLARE BANKRUPTCY?

This is not a question with an easy 'Yes' or 'No' answer, for the Bible does not directly address the issue. With so many people finding bankruptcy a necessary route it is important for any Christian contemplating this to consider how to apply Christian principles to their financial situation.

We have the responsibility to keep our promises and pay what we owe. Ecclesiastes 5: 4-5 says, "When you make a vow to God, do not delay in fulfilling it. He has no pleasure in fools; fulfil your vow. It is better not to vow than to make a vow and not fulfil it."

Bankruptcy is a serious matter and, at best, both sides lose. The creditors lose much of the money they are owed, and the debtors lose much of the respect they previously had. A person who has filed for bankruptcy can turn a negative situation into a positive one by making a commitment to repay what is legitimately owed. God's Word clearly says that a believer should be responsible for his or her promises and repay what is owed.

Larry Burkett

This principle is reiterated by Paul in Romans 13:8: "Let no debt remain outstanding." This verse does not prohibit the believer from incurring debts but it does suggest that when you do so you are entering into a legal agreement and spiritual commitment to repay the debt in a timely and honest manner.

Seeking bankruptcy or an IVA should not be considered lightly. Psalm 37:21 tells us: "The wicked borrow and do not repay, but the righteous give generously" and this surely applies to borrowing with no intent or no concerted effort to repay. However, in my opinion bankruptcy is permissible in three circumstances:

> *Do not withhold good from those who deserve it, when it is in your power to act. Do not say to your neighbour, "Come back later; I'll give it tomorrow" when you now have it with you.*
>
> **Proverbs 3:27-28**

1. Where a creditor forces a person into bankruptcy.

2. When the borrower experiences such extreme financial difficulties that there is no other option. There are occasions when the financial challenges become too extreme to reverse and bankruptcy is the only viable option. Even so, this option should be exercised only after all others have been explored.

> *Let no debt remain outstanding, except the continuing debt to love one another, for he who loves his fellowman has fulfilled the law.*
>
> **Romans 13:8**

3. If the emotional health of the borrower is at stake because of an inability to cope with the pressure of aggressive creditors.

For example, if a husband deserts his wife and children leaving her responsible for business or household debts, she may not have the resources or income to meet these obligations.

After a person goes through bankruptcy they should seek counsel from a competent solicitor to determine if it is legally permissible to repay the debt, even though they are not obliged to do so. If it is allowable, they should make every effort to repay it. For a large debt, this may be a long-term goal that is largely dependent upon the Lord supernaturally providing the resources. Your obedience here might allow God to show you favour in ways that you do not understand or expect: He really does bless obedience.

Thank you, Lord God, for giving us your biblical financial principles to keep us from the slavery of debt – and lead us into financial freedom – and I turn my heart to your ways. Thank you, Father, that you are righteous, just and compassionate – and if my choices/actions have, over time, brought me into debt – you also give us wisdom and counsel and a way forward to put things right. I do not want to be considered wicked – I want to be obedient to your word, face my responsibilities and keep my vows – help me to turn my financial anxieties into prayer and to listen and seek your answers for my situation. I choose to do right – Father take my hand and lead me through all the practical steps I need to take to put things right – and pay my debts – however long it takes. Thank you that I am never alone – that you have promised never to leave me or forsake me.
Amen

Advice
and counsel

DAY 15

Seeking wisdom

For lack of guidance a nation falls, but many advisers make victory sure.

Proverbs 11:14

There is no shortage of people who offer advice, whether it be government, voluntary organisations or businesses. Problems that advice agencies seek to address include such issues as debt, health, addictions and relationships. Some offer help and counsel while others offer follow on, paid-for services.

One couple who were experiencing marital difficulties felt they did not want others in the Church to know about their problems and so sought advice from a marriage guidance agency. After two visits and with little sign of reconciliation they were advised to divorce. Imagine the surprise and distress within the Church when they found that their former youth leaders were no longer married. And imagine how it felt for some of the former members of the youth group who had met at Church and subsequently married.

Listen to advice and accept instruction, and in the end you will be wise.

Proverbs 19:20

The Bible is not silent about where we should and should not seek counsel. The first four verses of Proverbs give insight into the purpose of the proverbs before the first proverb in chapter 1:5 tells the wise, "to listen and add to their learning, and let the discerning get guidance."

If we choose to take up what God desires to deposit in our lives through what He makes available in terms of wisdom, faith and prayer, we will have infinite resources.

WHAT IS WISDOM?

Wisdom is the practical use of knowledge; it is God giving something and you knowing what to do with it. It is the ability to discern God's hand in human circumstances and apply heavenly judgement to earthly situations. Wisdom is godly understanding – God's perspective given to us that allows us to take something that is complex and make it simple.

Whereas wisdom takes the complicated and simplifies it we often do the opposite – take what is simple and make it complicated! Wisdom takes our confusion and replaces it with clarity. It is the endowment of heart and mind that is needed for right conduct in life. Wisdom in the Bible is always accompanied by humility and the fear of the Lord. Corrie Ten Boom, a Christian holocaust survivor, said that God orders our steps and our stops. Sometimes it is wise to do just that: stop and apply God's resources to our lives.

So may we go from strength to strength,
And daily grow in grace,
Till in Your image raised at length,
We see You face to face.

LOOKING TO GOD

Paul instructs the believers at Ephesus: "I keep asking that the God of our Lord Jesus Christ, the glorious Father, may give you the Spirit of wisdom and revelation so that you may know Him better" (Ephesians 1:17).

I do not want the peace that passeth understanding. I want the understanding which bringeth peace.

Helen Keller, 1880-1968

It is a joy that God never abandons His children. He guides all who listen to His directions.

Corrie Ten Boom, Christian holocaust survivor

You have not lived until you have done something for someone who can never repay you.

John Bunyan

One of the purposes of trials is that you reach out and trust God and when the trial is over you will know Him better. Sometimes we may not understand what we are going through, but in such situations we should hear the voice of God telling us to ask Him. Sometimes we *look within* ourselves, at other times we *look around,* but the Bible encourages us to *look up* to get God's perspective.

My life is but a weaving
between my God and me
I cannot choose the colours
He weaveth steadily.
Oft' times he weaveth sorrow;
And I in foolish pride
Forget he sees the upper
And I the underside.
Not 'til the loom is silent
And the shuttle ceases to fly
Will God unroll the canvas
And reveal the reason why.
The dark treads are as needful
In the weaver's skilful hand
As the threads of gold and silver
In the pattern He has planned.
He knows, He loves, He cares;
Nothing this truth can dim.
He gives the very best to those
Who leave the choice to Him.

Grant Tullar, shoe clerk in a woollen mill and Methodist minister

This poem expresses the truth that in this life we will not always fully understand the particular blending of joys and woes because we see only the underside of the tapestry of life. Only when we get to eternity and we stand before Him will the canvas be turned over and to our eternal delight we will see what God has been doing.

It is believed that the first Bible book written was the book of Job. In Job 28:12-13 we hear Job in his discourse asking, "Where can wisdom be found? Where does understanding dwell? Man does not comprehend its worth." His answer in verse 28 is that wisdom comes from a fear of the Lord. The final part of verse 28 tells us that we must shun evil to put ourselves in a situation where we can hear God's perspective.

Solomon in Proverbs is instructing his sons and tells them how highly he regards wisdom when he says in Proverbs 4: 7 that, "wisdom is supreme; therefore get wisdom."

Where can wisdom be found? Where does understanding come from? Man does not comprehend its worth.

Matthew 5:6, KJV

Prayer - Paul's prayer for the Church
Lord God how this world needs Your wisdom –
the 'wisdom of the world' leads us astray into 'the pride of life'. Holy Spirit, You have said You will give us the words to speak when necessary – I lean on You to bring out of me the treasure of wisdom and knowledge planted in me from Your word and teaching, to bring simplicity to 'complicated' problems. To apply wisdom from You before I do anything or speak into any situation. I don't want my life to be a canvas of knots and tangles but a beautiful canvas woven by Your hands! Amen

Counsel

The way of a fool seems right, but a wise man listens to advice.

Proverbs 12:15

Yesterday we looked at the importance of seeking God's wisdom. Today we will consider what the Bible has to say about seeking counsel.

SEEKING COUNSEL

What prevents us from seeking counsel? There are two common reasons – pride and stubbornness. As for pride, our culture often perceives seeking advice as a sign of weakness. We are told, "Stand on your own two feet; you don't need anyone to help make your decisions for you." Stubbornness is characterised by positions such as, "Don't confound me with facts; my mind is already made up."

God encourages us to use a great gift He has provided for our benefit – godly counsel. In Proverbs 19:20 we read, "listen to advice and accept instruction, and in the end you will be wise." While Proverbs 12:15 says, "the way of a fool seems right to him, but a wise man listens to advice." And Proverbs 10:8 says, "the wise man is glad to be instructed, but a self-sufficient fool falls flat on his face" (TLB).

We seek counsel to gain insights, suggestions and alternatives that will assist us in making decisions from a godly perspective.

He that gives good advice, builds with one hand; he that gives good counsel and example, builds with both; but he that gives good admonition and bad example, builds with one hand and pulls down with the other.

Francis Bacon, English lawyer, 1561–1626

SOURCES OF COUNSEL

Scripture: What does the Bible have to say on a particular issue? The Psalmist wrote, "your laws are both my light and my counsellors," (Psalm 119:24, TLB) and further on in Psalm 119:98-100, "Your commands make me wiser than my enemies.... I have more insight than all my teachers, for I meditate on your statutes.... I have more understanding than the elders, for I obey your precepts."

> *Plans fail for lack of counsel, but with many advisers they succeed.*
>
> **Proverbs 15:22**

Expect great things from God; attempt great things for God!"

**William Carey,
English Baptist missionary, 1761-1834**

Proverbs tells us why counsel is so important because, "plans fail for lack of counsel" (15:22).

The Bible makes this remarkable claim about itself: "for the word of God is living and active. Sharper than any double-edged sword...it judges the thoughts and attitudes of the heart" (Hebrews 4:12). The truths in the Bible are enduring and timeless. If the Bible provides clear direction regarding a financial matter we have within us the knowledge to follow God's Word. If the Bible is not specific about an issue, we should subject our decision to the second source of counsel:

THE COUNSEL OF GODLY PEOPLE

"The mouth of the righteous man utters wisdom, and his tongue speaks what is just. The law of his God is in his heart; his feet do not slip" (Psalm 37:30-31). The Christian life is not one of independence from other Christians but of interdependence on one another. God has given each of us certain abilities and gifts, but He has not given any one person all the abilities that he or she needs to be most productive.

Your spouse: If you are married, the first person you need to consult is your spouse, and in so doing you should enhance your relationship. Be sure to avoid the trap of allowing a situation to become a source of strife and friction. Consulting your spouse also honours him or her and, when it comes to finances, helps each spouse plan and prepare for times ahead.

Your parents: If you are not married, parents are an important source of counsel. They have years of experience and they know you well.

Church leaders: Those to whom we look for spiritual guidance and direction.

Experienced people: If they are not Christian you may wish to share their counsel with those who are.

A multitude of counsellors: Ecclesiastes 4:9 tells us that two are better than one.

The counsel of the Lord: At all times it is important to refer back to the Lord the counsel you receive. After all, one of His names is Wonderful Counsellor.

Earthly goods are given to be used, not to be collected. Hoarding is idolatry.

Dietrich Bonhoeffer

COUNSEL TO AVOID

Avoid the counsel of the wicked. My definition of wicked for these purposes is, "one who lives in a manner that disregards or is against God."

These include fortune tellers, mediums, spiritualists and horoscopes.

Avoid biased counsel – that which is not partial or independent. When receiving financial advice, ask yourself these questions: "What stake does this person have in the outcome of my decisions? How does he or she stand to gain or lose from this decision?" If the adviser will profit, be cautious when evaluating his or her advice and always seek a second, unbiased opinion.

I will instruct you and teach you the way you should go; I will counsel you with my eye upon you.

Psalm 32:8, RSV

*Order my footsteps by Thy Word,
And make my heart sincere;
Let sin have no dominion, Lord,
But keep my conscience clear.*

Isaac Watts, Hymn writer, 1674-1748

AND FINALLY...

When you are making a decision it may be helpful to withdraw to a quiet place where you can draw on the resources from heaven – your faith, the Bible, and prayer.

Thank you, Father God, that you give us the checks and balances in our lives through the wisdom of your Word and also wise counsel. Help me, Father, before I dash off and do things, out of impatience or discontent – or just plain stupidity – that have eternal consequences, to stop and think and ask for your counsel – How will this action affect my walk with you? How will my actions affect my wallet/finances long and short term? How will this affect my family, friends, work colleagues, business partners? Will this bring glory to you or myself? Please bring those wise counsellors onto my 'radar' that I may ask their advice and stop and listen before making impulsive purchases, deals, investments... I don't want to be a stubborn fool! Amen

*I will instruct you and teach you
the way you should go;
I will counsel you with my eye
upon you.*

Psalm 32:8

3

Growing in generosity

Attitude in giving | The amount to give |
The human response

Attitude
in giving

Should you tithe?

How different our standard is from Christ's. We ask how much a man gives. Christ asks how much he keeps.

Hudson Taylor

Tithing is one of those practices that usually reveals a clear divide in understanding and view. You either tithe – give 10 per cent of your [gross] income to the Lord through the Church – or you do not. It is not possible to tithe five per cent – a tithe is 10 per cent.

Let me declare my own position and practice. Ever since I was taught tithing I have tithed – that is I have given 10 per cent of my gross income to the Church. Every time I have been interviewed on radio the question, 'Should a Christian tithe?' has been asked, so I know this is a subject that is of great interest.

I'M GOING TO THE COURTROOM

Some years ago I conducted an exercise in which I imagined I was both the prosecuting and defending barrister in a case before a jury: 'Is tithing required of a Christian?' I wrote about ten pages for the biblical case for tithing and about the same number against. At the end of the day I decided to read my papers for and against and put my case to the jury, who deliberated for the afternoon and then retired for the evening. The next day the jury returned to their seats. When asked by the judge for a verdict, the foreman explained

Money never stays with me. It would burn me if it did. I throw it out of my hands as soon as possible, lest it should find its way into my heart.

John Wesley

that the jury was hung – six for and six against!

The truth is, I fully understand and accept the biblical case for the tithe, but I also understand those who regard the verses advocating the tithe to be Old Testament law that is not categorically reiterated anywhere in the New Testament, particularly by either Paul or Jesus, both of whom had ample opportunity to clearly and unequivocally restate the tithe as central to New Testament teaching. The New Testament saints did not have the New Testament to go by when they ministered – they only had the Old Testament. Furthermore, no matter how many promises God has made (Old and New Testament), they are 'Yes' in Christ and that includes God's promise of blessing from Malachi chapter 3 with regard to tithing.

I do not know for certain, but I suspect that those who ask about the tithe probably do not tithe and therefore either have not thought about it or have thought about it and decided it was not necessary, desirable or affordable.

At the end of my imagining, I retired to my study concluding that I needed to ask for a retrial at which I would present new evidence.

I never would have been able to tithe the first million I ever made if I had not tithed on my first salary, which was about $1.50 a week.

J D Rockefeller

HERE ARE MY SUBMISSIONS FOR YOU [THE JURY] TO CONSIDER

Although 2 Timothy 3:16 tells us that the entire Bible is God inspired and profitable for teaching and training in righteousness I will build my case on the New Testament and, as directed by the judge, will not refer to those verses on tithing.

Giving 10 per cent isn't the ceiling of giving; it's the floor. It's not the finish line of giving; it's just the starting blocks.

First, ownership: Paul in 1 Corinthians 10:26 tells us that everything on the earth is the Lord's. This makes it clear that God owns not just 10 per cent, but 100 per cent! So it is not a question of giving God just 10 per cent – we are stewards who are responsible to the owner for the handling of *all* that he owns.

Second, example: In fulfilment of Old Testament prophecy God sent his Son, Jesus, born of a virgin to this earth, with the sole purpose of His having His life taken from him in the cruellest way by being crucified. He was innocent and died that we might all accept Him as our Saviour, and put our trust in Him as he gave us His Holy Spirit. Without doubt Jesus Christ is the finest example of a giver. There is no one who is remotely comparable to Him. As Christians we seek to be like Him and to follow Him and His example. In truth, none of us is more like Jesus than when we are giving.

Thirdly, God: When we die and go to heaven we will meet God, who will have something to say about the way we lived our lives. One thing He is certain not to say to us is that we gave too much to the Church or the poor!

Fourthly, Jesus: Fifteen per cent of Jesus' words are about money, wealth and possessions. He told the rich man to give 100 per cent of what he owned to the poor, while he commended the widow who gave to the treasury more than anyone else, as He knew she had put in everything she had to live on.

Fifthly, Paul: Paul wrote to the Church that they should give proportionally [the tithe is proportionate], cheerfully and sacrificially.

Paul also wrote to Timothy and instructed believers to, "set aside a sum of money in keeping with his income" (1 Corinthians 16:2).

Sixthly, New Testament: Every New Testament example of giving goes far beyond the tithe and none of the examples falls short of it. "All the believers were one in heart and mind. No one claimed that any of his possessions was his own, but they shared everything they had" (Acts 4:32). Yes, they gave everything because much grace was upon them all (Acts 4:33). You really are more blessed when you give than when you receive (Acts 20:35).

Seventh, investing: When you give generously back to God, you are investing in the lives of others. We are called to invest in giving to the poor and in spreading the gospel – Christians are going to heaven but there are millions of others who need to be reached. So, this is one investment that is secure and will not go down when the market does!

We give because we love God and others. We give because we desire God's blessing on our lives (Luke 6:38).

First things belong to God.
The first day of the week belongs to God.
The first hour of the day belongs to God.
The first portion of your income belongs to God.
When you make God first, He can help you

James MacDonald

It is now your decision. I believe we should give back to God what is His and that we should give 10 per cent of our income to His Church.

WHAT DOES GOD THINK IF I DON'T TITHE?

The issue is not a financial one. It is one of obedience. If God's Word commands us to tithe and we choose not to, we are disobeying God. How can God bless us financially, if we are not obedient to Him?

OLD TESTAMENT REFERENCES TO TITHING

Genesis 14:20
Abram gave God a tenth of everything

Leviticus 27:30-32
A tithe of everything is holy

Numbers 18:24,26,28
A tenth is an offering to the Lord

Deuteronomy 12:6,11,17
Bring your tithes to the Lord

Deuteronomy 14:22,23,28
Set your tithe aside

2 Chronicles 31:5,6,12
They gave a great amount – a tithe of everything

Nehemiah 10:37-38
The tithe is brought into the House of God

Nehemiah 12:44
They brought that which was required

Nehemiah 13: 5,12
All of Judah brought their tithes

Malachi 3: 8-10
Do not God of the tithe

NEW TESTAMENT
REFERENCES TO TITHING

Matthew 23:23
Do not neglect to tithe

Luke 16:12
Be trustworthy with someone else's property

Luke 18:12
I give a tenth of all I receive

Hebrews 7:5,6,8-9
Collect a tenth from the people

CONSIDER ALSO
THESE SCRIPTURES

Acts 20:35
It is more blessed to give than to receive

1 Corinthians 4:2
It is important to be faithful [in giving]

1 Corinthians 16:1-2
Set aside money according to your income

2 Corinthians 8:1-20
Be rich in generosity

1 Timothy 6:17-19
Be generous and willing to share

Once again Lord I am reminded that everything belongs to You, Lord God – I am a steward in your Kingdom. Lord, you want to reach the lost, the poor, the broken hearted, the underprivileged – and as your child I am your heart, mouth, eyes, ears, hands and feet in this world. I see that you love to give and you gave everything in your son Jesus. Because I love You, I want to be obedient with a generous heart towards You – who has given me everything. Help me to loose the strings of my heart and my purse in thankfulness, worship and service to you. As I step out in obedience and give, Holy Spirit, please fill me with your love and grace. Thank You for your blessings. Amen

Giving

DAY 18

For some, being called to give is like one whose heartbeat is faint, and yet by understanding God's heart and drawing closer to Him the Lord arouses in him or her the desire to give.

Giving is an act that few acquire naturally, but it is at the heart of God's purpose for us. Intense competition for our resources competes with the desire to give. Perhaps we do not give because time denies us the opportunity to plan what to give away, or perhaps a deep-rooted belief that 'what is mine is mine' prevents us. What emotions do you experience when you are asked to give – unspeakable joy or feeling put on the spot?

Giving is natural to God – He gave us the earth on which we live and He gave His only Son's life that we may enjoy His extended fellowship. He calls us to reciprocate and be givers – He calls us to be like His Son who gave more than anyone else has ever been asked to give.

I saw a survey in USA Today that asked people on an average income of $50,000 how much they thought they needed to be comfortable and enjoy their desired standard of living. The answer was $75,000. The same question was then asked of people with an

You're never more like Jesus than when you're giving.

Pastor Johnny Hunt, First Baptist, Woodstock, Atlanta, USA

income of $100,000 and their answer was $250,000! In other words, the more we have, the more we want. In some respects money is like seawater – the more you drink the thirstier you get. God's way of breaking the cycle of greed is giving. There will always be a need for us to be generous and to share the resources God has given us to reach out to others in need and to invest in what God is doing.

Those who use their money totally for self-satisfaction or hoard it for that elusive "rainy day" are just as financially bound in God's eyes as those in debt. A Christian cannot be within God's will and hoard money. Those who hoard try to rationalise their behaviour with arguments that contradict God's Word.

Larry Burkett

PLAN YOUR GIVING

How long do you spend planning what you intend to give? Remember that our bank statements and credit cards are theological evidence of our spiritual temperature. Are we giving because we love God and others? I have long concluded in my own life that giving is mostly about attitude – an attitude of heart towards God and of love and compassion toward others. Hell is a real place that is torture for all those who do not love the Lord – what can we do to play our part in sharing the good news?

Will we miss what we give? Never! Martin Luther said that he had held many things in his hands and had lost them all, but whatever he had placed in God's hand he still possessed. Maybe he was testifying to the truth we read in Proverbs 11:24-25, "There is one who scatters, and yet increases all the more, and there is one who withholds what is justly due, and yet it results only in want. The generous man will be prosperous, and he who waters will himself be watered" (NASB). We have so many opportunities to give, and as one of the richer nations on this earth – an island of plenty surrounded by a world of need – we should give.

If a pauper gives to God, he'll feel like a prince. If a prince doesn't give to God, he'll feel like a pauper.

Paul encourages us to give cheerfully (2 Corinthians 9:7) while Jesus encourages us to give extravagantly (Mark 14:3-9). Paul encourages us to give regularly (1 Corinthians 16:2), sacrificially (2 Corinthians 8:2-3), excellently (2 Corinthians 8:7), worshipfully (Acts 10:1-4), and proportionately 1 Corinthians 16:2; while Matthew urges us to give in secret (Matthew 6:4).

HE WHO GIVES RECEIVES

We should not give just to receive a blessing but give out of obedience and by doing so God will bless us. Some of the benefits of giving include:

He is no fool who gives what he cannot keep to gain what he cannot lose.

Jim Elliot

- Giving makes you more like Jesus

- Giving draws you closer to God

- Giving breaks the grip of materialism

The only investment I ever made which has paid consistently increasing dividends is the money I have given to the Lord.

James Kraft, Founder of Kraft Foods

- Giving strengthens your faith

- Giving is an investment in eternity

- Giving blesses you in return

- Giving enhances your contentment

PLACES TO GIVE

Here are two specific destinations:

1. To the local *Church* and Christian ministries. 1 Timothy 5:17 says, "The elders who direct the affairs of the Church well are worthy of double honour, especially those whose work is preaching and teaching."

2. To the *poor*. "All they asked was that we should continue to remember the poor, the very thing I was eager to do" (Galatians 2:10).

Should we give to secular charities and media appeals for disasters etc., and to TV sponsored charitable fund raising? This is one of those questions that frequently arises, to which I remind those enquiring that secular charities have the advantage of appealing to the whole population while normally only Christians give to Christian causes. Having said that, we should be led by the Spirit at all times.

When we give, we invest in the Kingdom of God but unlike ordinary investments, the value cannot go down; we cannot lose what we invest in eternity.

Our Father is a giver, and as you grow older in your faith you might ask yourself if this is an area that needs a fresh look, a fresh start. Start by asking the following questions:

How much more do you plan to give to bless others and invest in what God is doing? Do you give from leftovers or from the firstfruits? Does God really need your money?

What does God want more than your money? He wants your heart to turn to Him so He can bless you. God's motive in His command for us to give is not to benefit Him – it is to benefit us!

Giving – not to get back – but to grow! What an amazing principle, Lord God! I want to be willing and joyful in my giving – speak to my heart and mind where You see needs for me to give with your blessing – so that I may give generously from your generous provision to me. Bring maturity to my character, Holy Spirit, as you teach me about this. As I hear you and obey, my faith grows and I become more like Jesus – who gave everything to give me freedom. Forgive me, Lord, when I have given from wrong motives like pride, to be seen as 'a good person', to gain favour, or to make me feel better. I don't want to be selfish in my giving – but to grow in character, to be a channel for your blessing; to be content and close to You – the very best place to live! Amen

We should give...	Old Testament	New Testament
Generously	1 Chronicles 29:14-17; 2 Chronicles 31:5	Mark 14:3-9; 1 Timothy 6:17-19
Systematically	Genesis 28:16-22; Deuteronomy 14:22; Proverbs 3:9-10	1 Corinthians 16:1-2
Thoughtfully	Haggai 1: 3-11	2 Corinthians 8:2-3
Extravagantly	1 Chronicles 29:2-9; Ezra 2:69	Mark 12: 41-44; Mark 14:3-9 John 12: 1-8;
Reverently	Deuteronomy 14:23 Leviticus 22:20; Malachi 1:6-9	Matthew 2:11
Proportionately	Deuteronomy 16:17	1 Corinthians 16:2
Joyfully	2 Chronicles 24:10; and 29:31-36	2 Corinthians 8:2
Willingly	Exodus 35:21-22; 1 Chronicles 29:6	2 Corinthians 8:3
Regularly	Deuteronomy 16:16; Nehemiah 10: 35-39	1 Corinthians 16:2
Faithfully	Deuteronomy 14:27; 2 Chronicles 31:4-8	2 Corinthians 8:1-3
Expectantly	Genesis 28:20-22; Malachi 3:8-10	Luke 6:38; 2 Corinthians 9:6-11
Eternally	–	Matthew 6:19-20, Mark 10:21; Hebrews 11:13-16; 1 Timothy 6:19
Worshipfully	–	Acts 10:1-4
Secretly	–	Matthew 6:4
Cheerfully	–	2 Corinthians 9:7
Sacrificially	–	2 Corinthians 8:2-3
Excellently	–	2 Corinthians 8:7

The amount
to give

Good news for the poor

He who bestows his goods upon the poor shall have as much again and ten times more.

John Bunyan, Preacher, 1628 – 1688

Who do you think of when you think of the poor? Those on the street who sell magazines, those who beg or citizens of poor countries? Or perhaps individuals you know who live on low income or state benefit, or those who, for whatever reason, have 'lost everything' and now have to adjust to a very different lifestyle?

When most people think about the poor they think of those who do not have enough food, clothing or shelter. What about the people in the UK who are considered to be poor? Clearly most are not as needy as the ultra poor living in Africa and India, who surely should be on our radar when it comes to prayer and giving.

We might reflect on what is to blame for the plight of those in poverty and point to such things as capitalist exploitation, but this would be to disregard the contribution capitalism has made to advantage the poor.

We are an island of plenty surrounded by a world of need.

Similarly, we might point to the effects of social injustice, but it is equally important to reflect on ways in which society and government seek to provide basic care with dignity.

With a global population in the region of seven billion, more than two billion of whom are considered to be poor, we can feel nothing but awe and admiration for those who have been called to a lifetime of service to the poor.

What I kept I lost. What I spent I had. What I gave I have.

Persian Proverb

GOD WANTS US TO HELP THE POOR

The Bible reveals God's heart and concern regarding the poor in more than three hundred verses. Jesus said, "The poor you will always have with you, but you will not always have me" (Matthew 26:11).

The parable of the Good Samaritan in Luke 10:25-37 serves to remind us that we should reach out and help when we are able to. Ignoring those whom God calls us to minister to is not a Kingdom option.

Caring for the poor is a theme that resonates throughout Scripture. In the Old Testament in Deuteronomy we read, "Give generously to him and do so without a grudging heart; then because of this the Lord your God will bless you in all your work and in everything you put your hand to. There will always be poor people in the land. Therefore I command you to be open-handed towards your brothers and towards the poor and needy in your land" (Deuteronomy 15: 10-11).

Isaiah, the prophet, declares God's commands to extend care to the poor in Isaiah chapter 58:10-11 saying, "If you extend your soul to the hungry and satisfy the afflicted soul, then your light shall dawn in the darkness, and your darkness shall be as the noonday. The Lord will guide you continually, and satisfy your soul in drought,

The poorest man in the world is the man who has nothing but money.

He who gives to the poor will lack nothing, but he who closes his eyes to them receives many curses.

Proverbs 28:27

and strengthen your bones; you shall be like a watered garden, and like a spring of water, whose waters do not fail."

In the New Testament giving to the poor is emphasised by many of the writers, but Jesus and Paul in particular. For example, the rich man is condemned for not inviting Lazarus to his table or joining him at the gate (Luke 16:19-31).

A VISITOR

One evening my doorbell rang and there stood a beggar asking for food. My initial reaction was, 'Oh no,' but then I invited him in and gave him soup and food. While I was talking with him I was wondering where it might lead – would he keep coming back? My family sat in the living room wondering what I was doing. Now I wish I had welcomed him with more open arms and greater warmth, but I did not. I said to my family after he left that I had talked to him thinking that he could be Jesus – and in a sense he was.

He who is kind to the poor lends to the Lord, and he will reward him for what he has done.

Proverbs 19:17

I share this to demonstrate that we are not all strong in all areas of our lives. We all have tests but maybe we should see them as opportunities. I ask myself where are the poor in my budget? Will God be able to say to me one day what he said to King Josiah, '"He defended the cause of the poor and needy, and so all went well. Is that not what it means to know me?" Thus declares the Lord' (Jeremiah 22:16).

Father God – you do not want anyone living in poverty, but all of us in this world, by our selfishness and greed, have a part in producing poverty in individuals' lives. Forgive my nation for those damaging things it has done and unjust policies it has agreed to: and forgive me too for those times of not caring, taking what I have for granted and selfishness that have been a part of causing others to be poor. I want to be part of the answer, Father – open my eyes and help me have a sensitive heart towards those I meet who are poor in any way – not just financially poor but poor in soul and spirit – which can so often lead to financial poverty. Help me, Lord God, to adjust my thoughts and budget to include generosity in terms of my time and money to those in need. Amen

Laws of prosperity

Prosperity inebriates men, so that they take delights in their own merits.

John Calvin, French Theologian, 1509 - 1564

Prosperity, like tithing, is one of those topics that causes differences of opinion; and often people on both sides have strong views. I do not regard a focus on prosperity based on the belief that God is going to bestow great riches on oneself to be a healthy focus, although there are Christians who God *has* richly blessed. For me, to place the verses that talk about prosperity under a microscope without the balance of understanding about how we are to use that prosperity is to repeat the same failing that was in the heart and mind of the rich young ruler whose heart was governed by his wealth.

To define prosperity simply in terms of wealth is to deny a balanced approach to everything the Bible has to say about it. Here are seven 'laws' of prosperity that the Bible reveals in its own words:

THE LAW OF WISDOM

The highest wisdom resides in God's supreme thought and love. God allows us to obtain godly wisdom and He tells us to give this attention. Proverbs 23:4 says, "Do not wear yourself out to get rich; have the wisdom to show restraint." How do we obtain wisdom? James 1:5 says, "If any of you lack wisdom he should ask God, who gives generously to all without finding fault, and it will be given to him." Proverbs 9:10 and Psalm 111:10 tell us that fear of the Lord is the beginning of wisdom.

THE LAW OF PRIORITY

Enduring success can be achieved only when we prioritise in accordance with divine instruction – at all levels, including financial matters. We read in Joshua 1:8, "This Book of the Law shall not depart from your mouth, but you shall meditate in it day and night, that you may observe to do according to all that is written in it. For then you will make your way prosperous, and then you will have good success" (NKJV).

THE LAW OF MOTIVE

Meaningful work and living are motivated by unconditional love for others. In Proverbs 16:2 we read, "All the ways of a man are pure in his own eyes, but the Lord weighs the spirits" (NKJV). Further on in Proverbs 21:2 it says, "All the ways of a man seem right to him, but the Lord weighs the heart," while Proverbs 27:19 says, "As water reflects a face, so a man's heart reflects the man."

THE LAW OF GENEROSITY

Service and giving create abundance, both for others and ourselves. Matthew 6:21 says, "For where your treasure is, there your heart will be also." Proverbs 3:9 tells us to, "Honour

One more revival – only one more – is needed, the revival of Christian stewardship, the consecration of the money power to God. When that revival comes, the Kingdom of God will come in a day.

Horace Bushnell, Congregational minister 1802–1876

... always rejoicing; poor, yet making many rich; having nothing, and yet possessing everything.

2 Corinthians 6:10

Let temporal things serve your use, but the eternal be the object of your desire.

Thomas A Kempis,
Catholic monk,
1380 – 1471

the Lord with your wealth, with the firstfruits of all our crops" (which is what the tithe is – the first ten per cent); then your barns will be filled to overflowing, and your vats will brim over with new wine" (Proverbs 3:10). Proverbs 11:25 says, "A generous man will prosper; he who refreshes others will himself be refreshed," while Proverbs 19:17 counsels, "He who is kind to the poor lends to the Lord, and He will reward him for what he has done."

A wealthy Christian man who lost everything in a financial downturn was asked if he ever regretted all he had given to the Lord's work. He replied, "What I gave, I still have. What I kept, I lost."

THE LAW OF UNDERSTANDING

To be able to love with God's heart we need to see through His eyes and think His thoughts, for these are the ultimate goals for the truly enlightened spirit. Luke 11:34 says, "Your eye is the lamp of your body. When your eyes are good, your whole body also is full of light. But when they are bad, your body also is full of darkness." Paul in Colossians 1:9 says, "For this reason, since the day we heard about you, we have not stopped praying about you and asking God to fill you with the knowledge of his will through all spiritual wisdom and understanding." That is a great prayer model and certainly one we should pray for anyone whom we counsel. The Psalmist asks God to, "Show me your ways, O Lord, teach me your paths; guide me in truth and teach me" (Psalm 25:4-5).

THE LAW OF PREPARATION

Being responsible with and wisely managing life's resources requires commitment to truly important purpose and careful planning. Luke 16: 11 says, "Therefore if you have not been faithful in the use of worldly wealth, who will entrust the true riches to you?" (NASB). Paul in 1 Corinthians 4:2 says, "Moreover, it is required of stewards, that a man be found faithful," (NKJV) while in 2 Timothy 2:21 Paul says, "If a man cleanses himself from the latter [avoiding worldly and empty chatter], he will be an instrument for noble purposes, made holy, useful to the Master and prepared to do any good work."

Now he who supplies seed to the sower and bread for food will also supply and increase your store of seed and will enlarge the harvest of your righteousness.

2 Corinthians 9:10

THE LAW OF PRESERVATION

Wise stewardship ensures that money principles, values, and spiritual guidance can be passed from one generation to the next. Psalm 25:21 says, "May integrity and uprightness protect me, because my hope is in you." 1 Thessalonians 5:23 tells us, "May God himself, the God of peace, sanctify you through and through. May your whole spirit, soul and body be kept blameless at the coming of our Lord Jesus Christ."

As we seek prosperity in body, mind, and spirit we will be drawn closer to God and understand more fully His will for our life.

Blessed are all who fear the Lord, who walk in his ways. You will eat the fruit of your labour; blessings and prosperity will be yours.

Psalm 128:1-2

Father God, you've planned prosperity for us your children, but it's far more than just about money – it's my whole being You want me to prosper. For me to live my life in tune with you – I constantly need your help. I praise you for sending your Holy Spirit to empower and equip me with every spiritual blessing to overcome all my temptations, wrong thinking and bad habits – all those parts of me that hinder me from flowing in your blessing. I come to you, Father God, with an open heart and mind – please fill me now to overflowing with your Holy Spirit that I may constantly be learning, understanding and putting into practise your way of living a whole, prosperous life with financial freedom – not just for my comfort or benefit alone but to be a good steward in your Kingdom, generous in my giving and a good example to those people you place around me and whose paths I cross on my journey through life. Amen

The human response

Work and business

I enjoyed a career managing my own businesses for over 30 years. I had no formal business training and my only qualification was a professional one. Back when I started my first business, there were relatively few self-help books on managing a business so I learned to apply biblical management principles to my understanding of how to grow my business.

If you are a business owner or manager the Bible is replete with wisdom and principles that apply to how you manage and grow a business. After all, Jesus' earthly father was in business on his own account, and Jesus certainly grew up with the dynamics of business around him before he went full-time into "My Father's business."

A business owner or manager can apply the principles in this devotional to managing a business. For example, if you are in business - God is the owner (1 Chronicles 29:11-12). Indeed that is a very good place to start, as I know what it is like to see the business as *mine*!

There are four primary purposes for a business:

1. TO GLORIFY GOD

Business owners and managers should glorify God in their personal and business lives. In John 17:4, Jesus said, "I have brought you [God the Father] glory on earth by completing the work you gave me to do." The only way to glorify the Lord is to conduct our business according to the principles found in God's Word. Our work must be done without compromising God's ways.

Glorifying God in the business means dealing with employers, employees, suppliers, customers, and competitors as if we were dealing with Christ. Christian business leaders try to build win-win relationships, not just because it is good business practice, but because they care about other people. Besides glorifying God it also earns us the right to introduce others to the Saviour.

The secret of your success is determined by your daily agenda...we over exaggerate yesterday, we overestimate tomorrow and we underestimate today.

John Maxwell

2. TO SERVE THE NEEDS OF ITS CUSTOMERS

One of the greatest privileges we have is to be able to serve others. Jesus' life was an overwhelming commitment to serving and blessing others. When I lecture professionals on management I often ask this question, "What is the purpose of the business?" The overwhelming response is, "to make a profit." That is for the Christian however, the wrong answer. As Christians we are called to serve one another - and that includes those who are called to business. As we will consider at the end of this study - profit is an outcome of serving the customers of the business. Focus on the pursuit of making money and we run the risk of letting money take control of our hearts. For a non Christian business owner this must surely be the first objective of the

All hard work brings a profit, but mere talk leads only to poverty.

Proverbs 14:23

Come to me, all who labour and are heavy laden, and I will give you rest.

Matthew 11:28, RSV

Business tithing is not dramatically different from personal tithing. However, calculating a business tithe is not necessarily as clear-cut as calculating your personal tithe. You should tithe on business increase, which may not be the same as gross, because you are dealing with non-cash assets as well as stocks. Only in prayer can you decide how best to honour the Lord through your business.

Larry Burkett,
Co-Founder,
Crown Financial
Ministries, 1939-2003

business but for a Christian business owner glorifying God must come first.

For a Christian business owner there is often the opportunity to be a blessing to others and maybe allow some of our giving to be channelled through the business.

3. TO SUPPORT THE WORK OF CHRIST

There is a dependent relationship between those involved in Christian ministry and Christians in business – they need one another. This is not an accidental relationship; God designed it that way.

Paul wrote to the Roman Church, "Having then gifts differing according to the grace that is given to us, let us use them: if prophecy, let us prophesy in proportion to our faith; or ministry, let us use it in our ministering...he who gives, with liberality" (Romans 12:6-8, NKJV).

Giving is one of the purposes of Christians in business; it is what God has gifted them to do. When businessmen and women understand that they are strategic in contributing to the funding of the work of Christ, their work takes on eternal significance.

4. TO SPIRITUALLY IMPACT YOUR SPHERE OF INFLUENCE

The Lord has given business owners and managers a position of influence in the workplace to impact co-workers, suppliers, customers, and even competitors. If you count the family members of everyone you impact, you may have a larger 'congregation' than many churches.

The Lord has appointed business owners to represent Him and bring His principles, values, love and presence into the workplace. The workplace provides a platform for evangelism, for discipleship, and for influencing others through serving and then sharing His message through words and actions.

The Bible has so much to say about running a business including leadership, finances, human resources, organisation, planning and marketing. We all serve an amazing God. You might not be a business owner or manager yourself but you can pray for those you know who are. Business owners have responsibilities and opportunities – pray that they may use them to extend His Kingdom here on earth.

> *It is our best work that He wants, not the dregs of our exhaustion. I think He must prefer quality to quantity.*
>
> **George MacDonald, Poet and Scottish Minister 1824-1905**

5. TO MAKE A PROFIT

We looked at number two at the fact that meeting the needs of customers is the number one important purpose after glorifying God. So, what about profitability? One of the outcomes of a business is to make a profit. There is no biblical admonition against making a profit. Profits are the result of a well-run business and should be considered both normal and honourable.

Unfortunately, there are many reasons why businesses fail to earn a profit. Some are unprofitable because they lack effective internal controls, some are disorganised, some are unable to attract good employees, some do not understand changes in their customers' needs, and some see their results slump due to external causes such as a recession.

Some businesses are not profitable because the owners choose to live beyond the means of their business. They go out of business because the owner draws a salary larger than the business can afford.

The commitment to being profitable means wisely building a business with a solid foundation and not allowing greed or presumption to put employees, investors, suppliers or creditors at undue risk. Although it is no sin to fail in business, business owners and managers should seek to conduct their business in ways that promote financial stability.

Thank you Lord for the opportunities to work for you. I am thankful that you are my ultimate boss. I thank you that you care for me, encourage me, discipline me, direct me and open doors at the right time. I thank you that you provide for me to use the skills and talents you have given me. Thank you Lord, although there always seems so much to do, but I will not feel guilty taking time to rest – help me to find my rest in you – even as I work. Amen

There is a time for everything, and a season for every activity under heaven.

Ecclesiastes 3:1

DAY 21

4

Save.
Invest.
Spend.

Income exceeds expenses | Lifestyle |
Perspective

Income exceeds expenses

DAY
22

Building godly integrity

The integrity of the upright guides them, but the unfaithful are destroyed by their duplicity.

Proverbs 11:3

The Oxford dictionary defines integrity as, 'the quality of being honest and having strong moral principles.'

The word 'integrity' appears sixteen times in the King James Bible. The first two references are in Genesis 20:5-6, where Abimelech tells God that he believes that Sarah was Abraham's sister and that he was free to sleep with her. Abimelech refers to the integrity of his heart before God affirms that he sought to act with honesty of heart. The next reference in 1 Kings 9:4-5 finds God counselling Solomon to walk in integrity of heart as one of the conditions for establishing "your royal throne over Israel forever," thus fulfilling the promise God made to David. The remaining instances appear in the three books of the Bible known as the Wisdom literature: Job, Psalms and Proverbs.

EMBRACING INTEGRITY

There is something in the character of integrity that we should take hold of. The character of a Christian should embrace integrity because it is an essential trait found in godly upright people. As Proverbs 11:3 makes clear, integrity guides us. The second part of the verse contrasts integrity with its absence, which results in destruction!

How does integrity apply to how you use your money, wealth and possessions? You should seek to be honest in all your financial dealings – honest with yourself, with others and above all before God. You should seek to do what needs to be done, when it needs to be done and how it needs to be done; giving back to God, dealing rightly and on a timely basis with those to whom we owe money, living in such a way that your expenditure does not exceed your income, and in your heart acknowledging that God is the owner of all.

Your godly integrity provides a rudder that guides you in handling your finances as it aligns your heart, thoughts and deeds.

It is important to give due diligence to all the talents God has given. Maybe you have two talents that you can treble? Our character develops and matures as we address and engage in dealing with situations that need to be left behind – maybe a poor financial decision, maybe a decision taken on impulse. We must learn to forgo the lures of this world.

INTEGRITY'S CHARACTER TRAITS

Integrity consists of two character traits – the first knows the difference between right and wrong (no wonder this goes hand in glove with righteousness!) and the second applies that knowledge and does what is right. This requires discipline, which is like a tributary that includes integrity as it feeds into our character. Having a commitment to sustaining and developing our integrity is important because it is an essential part of our walk of faith and avoiding wrong

God looks at the heart, not the hand – the giver, not the gift.

My worth to God in public is what I am in private.

Oswald Chambers

And when Simon saw that through the laying on of the apostles' hands the Holy Spirit was given, he offered them money, saying, "Give me this power also, that anyone on whom I lay hands may receive the Holy Spirit." But Peter said to him, "Your money perish with you, because you thought that the gift of God could be purchased with money!

Acts 8:18-20

decisions and situations that cause us to fall short of God's best for our lives. The Psalmist, describing a man of integrity said, "He whose walk is blameless, and who does what is righteous, speaks the truth from his heart...keeps his oath [to repay debts] even when it hurts..." (Psalm 15:2, 4). Avoiding pain is a far better option than unnecessary pain and struggle.

Do all the good you can, by all the means you can, in all the ways you can, in all the places you can, at all the times you can, to all the people you can, as long as you can.

John Wesley

ENJOYING PROSPERITY

In order to enjoy a whole life of prosperity we should seek to develop godly integrity, and then make sure we apply this aspect of our character especially in how wealth is acquired and used. As we discover what we believe, we may need to adapt and align our beliefs no matter the cost. It is sometimes easy to sidestep our integrity if we feel the cost is too high. As Abimelech learnt, God wants us to live with integrity of heart. We see this in the story of Abraham and Abimelech in Genesis 20. God literally saved Abimelech from death because of his integrity after Abraham lied to him. Our integrity will guide us, "The integrity of the upright guides them, but the unfaithful are destroyed by their duplicity" (Proverbs 11:3).

When Jesus saw Nathanael approaching, he said of him, "Here is a true Israelite, in whom there is nothing false."

John 1:47

Stand up! Stand up for Jesus!
The strife will not be long;
This day the noise of battle,
The next the victor's song.
To those who vanquish evil
A crown of life shall be;
They with the King of glory
Shall reign eternally.
George Duffield, Jr., 1818-1888

Father, I do not want to be compromised for lack of integrity – I want and need financial freedom and here I am again seeing how much knowing and applying Your Word to every part of my being is the way to develop integrity. Help me to always have integrity and not be drawn into applying the accepted standards of our day – which are so often far from Your own. I want to be known as a person who has integrity in all my financial dealings – paying my bills on time, never cheating. What they see is what they get – always! – Open, honest and trustworthy – no double standards! Help me, Lord, when the world lures me into wanting something and getting it anyway I can, and at any cost to my soul and my finances – help me to pause and use integrity as my guide. Amen

DAY 23

Being content

Spend less than you earn and do it for a long time and you will be financially successful.

**Ron Blue,
Kingdom Advisors**

The global financial crisis in 2008 changed many people's fortunes and view of their finances. Those in retirement saw their income from savings diminish while those paying their mortgage benefitted from lower interest rates. But the burden of unsecured debt remained costly as rates on this lending hardly reduced. For many, then as maybe now, their spending was considerably greater than their income.

In 2 Kings 4, we learn about the widow who sought to recover from the loss of her husband. She was faced with the challenge of losing her sons to those creditors who had been instructed to recover the debts left by her husband. She turned to Elisha the prophet and, in spite of his surprising advice to find and fill jars with her oil, she obeyed. The result? Her debts repaid and a household enjoying financial recovery.

We may wonder what she spent the money on or what her children asked her to buy, but whatever her circumstances, families in Bible times did not have supermarkets with tens of thousands of items from which to select or the Internet with its easy-to-buy online purchasing systems – nor did they have to face adverts at every turn!

If we are not to fall into the trap of being a 'slave to the lender,' we must give serious consideration to planning what we spend, not extending secured borrowing to the limit, and reducing any unsecured debt.

Then some soldiers asked him, "And what should we do?" He replied, "...be content with your pay."

Luke 3:14

START MAKING A PLAN

Whatever your income and expenditure, having a financial plan should be a priority. Self-control starts with developing a realistic and balanced income and expenditure plan that you can use to introduce discipline into your spending – especially where you might be tempted to spend beyond your means. Creating a plan is the first important step to getting control of your finances. If you have 'no problem' with your monthly finances maybe you could look at your giving, or even at how you might reduce your outgoings. If you are having difficulty make sure you are not heading towards the day when the threatening letter arrives!

Never spend your money before you have it.

Thomas Jefferson

It is important to take time to record and analyse your income and expenditure, being sure to record all payments whether through your bank account, card accounts or cash.

Next make a list of everything you owe – is there anything overdue?

Finally, look at the number of cards in your wallet or purse. If any of them has money outstanding for more than two months the card is not serving you, you are serving the card company – and probably paying them at least 18 per cent interest!

You should complete the remaining daily studies before finalising your spending plan.

I am always content with what happens, for I know that what God chooses is better than what I choose.

Epictetus, Greek philosopher, 55AD – 135AD

Meanwhile, take some time to study your expenditure patterns and think about what you can reduce or eliminate. Pray through how you handle your finances and, like the widow and her plea to the prophet, call out to God and ask Him for his wisdom and help.

LEARNING TO BE CONTENT

The apostle Paul wrote in 1 Timothy 6:8, "if we have food and covering [clothes and shelter], we will be content with that." But, our consumer-society does not want us to be content. Are there elements of your spending where you are conformed to the ways of this world? For example, a mobile phone is now deemed an absolute necessity and yet the monthly cost can easily be £30 or more; and cable television with its hundreds of channels is regarded as a household essential in many homes. Again, Paul wrote in Philippians 4:11-13, "I have learned to be content whatever the circumstances. I know what it is to be in need and I know what it is to have plenty. I have learned the secret of being content in any and every situation, whether well fed or hungry, whether living in plenty or in want."

Paul learned to be content. He was not born with this instinct and neither are we; we must intentionally develop it.

AVOID COVETING

Coveting means craving someone else's property, and Scripture prohibits it. The last of the Ten Commandments is, "You shall not covet your neighbour's house. You shall not covert your neighbour's wife, or his

God can have our money and not have our hearts, but he cannot have our hearts without having our money.

R Kent Hughes

manservant or maidservant, his ox or donkey, or anything that belongs to your neighbour." We could paraphrase this commandment to read: "Do not allow your eyes and mind to stray to other women or men, or to anyone who is married; and do not desire to have a car or house like theirs, the technology they have, or holidays like they take."

We should not use comparison to justify spending more than we should. Many people have suffered financially because they insisted on 'keeping up with the Joneses' even though they could not afford to. Someone once said, "You can never keep up with the Joneses. Just when you thought you'd caught up, they go deeper into debt to buy more stuff!"

And I - in righteousness I will see your face; when I awake, I will be satisfied with seeing your likeness.

Psalm 17:15

Father God, thank you that no matter how I get into any financial problems if I turn my life around to You, You will provide a way forward - like You did for the widow. Forgive me when I have been discontent, jealous and coveted possessions. Help me Lord to discipline myself and face these issues now and take an honest look at why, how and what I'm spending my income on. When I get fearful about all this - help me to keep living in Your love which dispels all fear and to persevere with my plan to reach financial freedom. Amen

Investing principles from Psalm 23

David's Psalm 23 is perhaps the best known Psalm and one that has been a source of comfort and inspiration for millions. So let us lie down and allow Him to lead us beside still waters.

While there are 2,350 Bible verses dealing with money and possessions, there are other passages that on first examination do not seem to speak about money but from which we can draw biblical financial principles. Psalm 23 is one of those passages.

THE LORD IS MY SHEPHERD

A shepherd's calling is to guide and protect his flock. As far as the New Testament is concerned Jesus never called himself a priest, a preacher, or an elder, but liked to think of himself as a shepherd. He had many metaphors by which he revealed his character, but the one he loved best to paint his portrait with was shepherd. Now, if He is our shepherd, we are His sheep.

While I was living in Atlanta my [adult] Sunday School leader, who is a sheep farmer, taught me some interesting things about sheep. He said that sheep are dumb creatures that often stray but are defenceless because they have no speed, strength or savvy. Sheep are also totally dependent!

We have a shepherd who is our master. He is the one we look to as guide and protector. In John 3:16 we learn how he died to save us. Proverbs 3:6 says, "If we acknowledge him he will make our paths straight," and Psalm 37:4 says, "Delight yourself in the Lord and he will give you the desires of your heart."

So, the first investment lesson from this Psalm is to invest our lives in Jesus as Shepherd – and King, not allowing money or any other idol to be our master (Matthew 6:24).

The plans of the diligent lead surely to abundance, but every one who is hasty comes only to want.

Proverbs 21:5, RSV

I SHALL NOT BE IN WANT

The world and the flesh always urge us to want more and better. Whatever returns you gain on your investments they are never enough! As the world influences us to live in a continual state of want we incur debt or work longer hours. Paul learnt the lesson of Psalm 23 when in 1 Timothy 6 he wrote to Timothy telling him that his needs were for food, shelter and clothing – anything over and above are wants. In Philippians 4:11, Paul tells the Church at Philippi that he has, "learned to be content whatever the circumstances."

Your heavenly Father knows what you need for tomorrow and He can direct you to investments that meet your future needs.

HE MAKES ME TO LIE DOWN IN GREEN PASTURES

The world says there are greener pastures somewhere other than where the Lord has led you. In the investment arena we see adverts for a myriad of investments, all claiming to

If we command our wealth, we shall be rich and free; if our wealth commands us, we are poor indeed. We are bought by the enemy with the treasure in our own coffers.

Edmund Burke,
Irish statesman

offer a better, greener pasture in performance and results. Many of these are nothing more than dead straw and not the green pasture promised in Scripture. The dead grass of financial bondage, materialism, covetousness and constant drive for more, and the dead grass of unfulfilment when we attain all the things we think will make us happy and contented.

Can they really fulfil these promises? If the Lord is your shepherd, He can guide you in the choice of investments and investment advisers to a green pasture of His choosing.

HE LEADS ME BESIDE STILL WATERS

Still or quiet waters can be compared to a more restful, more tranquil, investment strategy. Conservative, or moderate, investment portfolios may not have the high returns promised by aggressive or speculative investing, but they are usually safer and quieter. Investments with higher returns are like turbulent waters – more volatile and with higher risk of loss.

The last twenty years of the 20th century and the two decades of the current century have demonstrated all too clearly that investments go down as well as up. We have seen times of great turbulence. In the same way that earthquakes can be 'sort of' predicted, so too can market falls. The reality is that most of the time no-one really knows when or by how much it will fall. The Psalm 23 philosophy leads me to look at conservative, or moderate, investment strategies that enable me to be calm beside still waters and stay away from those that rage.

Even Christians find themselves distressed when stock markets crash. Matthew 6: 19-20 provides a spiritual reality check that we should not, "lay up for yourselves treasures on earth, where moth and rust destroy and where thieves break in and steal; but lay up [invest] for yourself treasures in heaven..."

If anyone does not provide for his relatives, and especially for his immediate family, he has denied the faith and is worse than an unbeliever.

1 Timothy 5:8

Thank you Jesus, that you are the Good Shepherd, that when we follow You, you lead us to safe places where you protect and care for us, look over us daily, tend and heal our wounds and provide us with refreshing water and sustenance for the day. As I come under your shepherding with my income, lead me to places of wisdom and safety in which to invest my 'talent' or money in. Teach me to be secure in You and not my 'talent' so that even if the return falls or fails, I know You will still provide for my needs each day. I do not need the 'excitement' of the quick gain and in this world that is constantly shouting at me – you need this! Buy that! I need your quiet waters and my soul restored – lead me on Good Shepherd. Amen

Financial planning

Failing to [prayerfully] plan is [potentially] planning to fail.

Mark Lloydbottom

It is rightly said that failing to plan is planning to fail. I always view God as the ultimate planner, and the Bible is replete with His plans for man. He has set clear goals for man, his redemption and his life on this earth and in eternity. He has provided us with what we need to live and reproduce. God has had a plan for each of us from the beginning.

When President Kennedy announced that America was going to land man on the moon by the end of the 1960s the whole nation was galvanised and motivated by the space race and the desire to achieve that goal.

Can you remember watching athletes being interviewed after an Olympic event? While some might announce they are retiring most tell how they wish to return and improve their performance in four years time.

Vision and dreams are powerful motivators for both nations and individuals. Add to the mix instruction and godly wisdom from the Bible and you have all you need to achieve your godly financial goals.

What are the key areas where you should plan? Your response to that question will be personal to you and dependent on your situation and maybe how your thinking has evolved during these studies.

LOOK AT YOUR CURRENT SITUATION: MONTHLY INCOME AND EXPENDITURE

Do you have more income than expenditure? If not, then look at your expenditure to see where this can be reduced? What are you spending that could be stopped or reduced? Could you and should you earn more money?

The plans of the diligent lead surely to abundance, but every one who is hasty comes only to want.

Proverbs 21:5, RSV

DEBT

Is your total debt manageable within your budget? Resolve not to allow your debt to increase one penny more. Cut your cards up if that will help. This is one form of plastic surgery that over time will improve how you feel – and maybe even how you look! Use the snowball strategy – start by repaying the smallest debt first and then when this is repaid roll over the money you pay off this debt to the next smallest debt, and so on. Keep this process in place until each and every debt is repaid including educational loans, car loans, and home mortgages.

Your mortgage – if you move, is it really necessary to increase the mortgage? Perhaps you could reduce the term of the mortgage by two to five years? If the interest rate increases in less than five years could your finances cope with an increase of just two percentage points? Why not start saving that margin to prove that you are in control of your finances?

GIVING

Is giving a priority for you? Do you give from what is left over or out of your firstfruits?

"Honour the Lord with your wealth, with the firstfruits of all your crops" (Proverbs 3:9). This is repeated in Exodus 23:19: "Bring the best of the firstfruits of your soil to the house of the Lord your God." Remember that you are never more like Jesus than when you are giving, so be generous. Paul encourages us to give proportionately. You are the steward of all that has been entrusted to you. Remember that a tithe is ten per cent of income and that is certainly proportionate to your income. But remember also that it is not just ten per cent that belongs to God – it all belongs to Him. How much are you going to give to the Lord through your Church? Will you give to the poor? Do you have some money from which you could give when a need arises?

You've heard of prayer warriors. What about giving warriors? God has entrusted us with so much. Perhaps He is raising up a great army of givers, and He's calling us all to enlist.

Randy Alcorn

SAVING

Fluctuating interest rates and stock market falls have historically changed the forward planning of many people. Make sure you have some savings to protect your finances from being knocked off balance by the unexpected, and make a long-term commitment to saving. Perhaps in this way you could serve the Lord full-time sooner rather than later.

Record your answers to these questions and take the opportunity to write down a plan. Where could you add a little stretch into your planning? Ask God to lead you as you record what you sense are the right steps for you to take with your finances. If you are married, share finances and decisions with your spouse. This is one of those areas where couples can share together as they seek to manage what God has given.

JAMES ON THE FUTURE

"Now listen, you who say, 'Today or tomorrow we will go to this or that city, spend a year there, carry on business and make money.' Why, you do not even know what will happen tomorrow. What is your life? You are a mist that appears for a little while and then vanishes. Instead, you ought to say, 'If it is the Lord's will, we will live and do this or that.' As it is, you boast and brag. All such boasting is evil" (James 4:13-16).

Thank you, Father, that I have the security of knowing you have a plan for my life! What is wonderful, is that you want me to be involved in that plan – I'm not just a puppet on a string! There are things you want me to think about and do in order for your plan to unfold in life unhindered by sin. As I look at the years that have passed already, I realise I have not always been in tune

with your plan – forgive me for the times I have deviated into my own ways. I want to be totally honest – Holy Spirit help me to not deceive myself by thinking I'm all OK that everything is just fine! Now, as I write my plan give me your creativity, remind me of those unfulfilled dreams I still have – show me the truth of my financial position...where to tighten the belt, how to get out of any debt, where to expand my giving – keep me 'real' as I write, that my plan will bless you and become a blessing for me, my family and others. You are wonderful Father God! Amen

Lifestyle

DAY 26

Staying honest in all things

Do not steal. Do not lie. Do not deceive one another.

Leviticus 19:11

While many recognise that honesty in what is said and done is a standard to live by, others struggle with being honest. Handling our finances requires honesty with ourselves and to others. Have you ever been tempted not to pay for something or to pick up something that does not belong to you? At work or in business have you ever been tempted not to be truthful when trying to sell something?

While you may regard yourself as an essentially honest person we are all engaged in a battle between flesh and spirit. In Genesis after Noah and his family had made their first burnt sacrifice on dry ground the Lord said that He would not curse the ground because of man, "even though every inclination of his heart is evil from childhood" (Genesis 8:21). When Jesus explained the meaning of a parable He said that, "...those things which proceed out of the mouth come from the heart, and they defile a man. For out of the heart proceed evil thoughts, murders, adulteries, fornications, thefts, false witness, blasphemies" (Matthew 15:18-19, NKJV).

That's quite a list of daunting characteristics to avoid our thoughts and minds succumbing to! While our study time

here focuses on our finances, the full extent
of the practice of honesty reaches into many
areas of our lives.

HONESTY – A GODLY STANDARD

Truthfulness is one of God's attributes.
He is repeatedly identified as the God of
truth. "I am...the truth" (John 14:6); "speaks
the truth from the heart" (Psalm 15:2) and
"does his neighbour no harm" (Psalm 15:3)
are underlying fundamental requirements
in obeying the Ten Commandments. The
eight and ninth commandments instruct us:
"You shall not steal. "You shall not bear false
witness against your neighbour" (Exodus 20:
15-16, NKJV). Leviticus 19:11 restates these
commandments instructing us, "Do not
steal. Do not lie. Do not deceive one another."
Our society imprisons those who commit
'serious' acts of theft – but which of us has not
stolen something that belongs to another – a
writing pen, a postage stamp, or work time?
Ananias and Sapphira died because they
were dishonest – and they lied to the Apostles
about something that actually belonged to
them!

ESCAPING THE TEMPTATION OF DISHONESTY

Paul in his letter to the Galatian Church
instructed Christians to, "Live by the Spirit,
and you will not gratify the desires of the
sinful nature. For the sinful nature desires
what is contrary to the Spirit and the Spirit
what is contrary to the sinful nature"
(Galatians 5:16-17). The desire of the Spirit

*There is no twilight zone
of honesty in business.
A thing is right or it's
wrong. It's black or it's
white.*

John Dodge,
Car manufacturer,
1864-1920

The most important things in life aren't things and the best things in life are always free.

is for us to be honest. The absolutely honest life is supernatural – "God is spirit, and his worshipers must worship in spirit and in truth" (John 4:24). We need to submit ourselves entirely to Jesus Christ as Lord and allow Him to live His life through us. There is no other way.

Scripture teaches us to avoid the company of dishonest people because they influence those with whom they associate.

Never allow yourself to be trapped into anything that is unethical, immoral or dishonest, no matter how inviting it seems. There are no small lies – just lies. There are no small thefts – just thefts. A Christian's usefulness to God is directly proportional to his or her honesty.

**Larry Burkett, Co-Founder
Crown Financial Ministries, 1939-2003**

THE REMEDY FOR DISHONESTY

Unfortunately we sometimes slip and act dishonestly. Once we recognise it we need to act to restore our relationship with God. 1 John 1:9 tells us that, "If we confess our sins, he is faithful and just and will forgive us our sins and purify us from all unrighteousness." We should agree with God that our dishonesty was sin and then thankfully accept His gracious forgiveness so we can again enjoy His fellowship.

Restore your relationship with the harmed person, even if your dishonesty was only a boast or any other form of untrue account. James, Jesus' half brother who was converted after the resurrection, wrote that we should, "confess our sins to each other" (James 5:16). We cannot disobey God by practising dishonesty. Failing to confess and restore relationships may result in a lack of financial prosperity: "He who conceals his sins will not prosper, but he who confesses and forsakes them will obtain mercy" (Proverbs 28:13, RSV).

If anything has been acquired dishonestly it should be returned to its rightful owner, "Then it shall be, when he sins and becomes guilty, that he shall restore what he took by robbery...or anything about which he swore falsely; he shall make restitution for it in full and add to it one-fifth more. He shall give it to the one to whom it belongs" (Leviticus 6:4-5, NASB).

Restitution is a tangible expression of repentance and an effort to correct wrong. Zacchaeus is a good example. He promised Jesus, "if I have cheated anybody out of anything, I will pay back four times the amount" (Luke 19:8).

The Lord detests lying lips, but he delights in men who are truthful.

Proverbs 12:22

LET'S LOOK IN PROVERBS FOR THE PROMISED REWARDS FOR THOSE WHO ARE HONEST

Blessing of a more intimate relationship with the Lord: "for the Lord detests a perverse man but takes the upright into his confidence" (Proverbs 3:32).

An honest man is the noblest work of God.

**Alexander Pope,
1688-1744**

So that you will prove yourselves to be blameless and innocent, children of God above reproach in the midst of a crooked and perverse generation, among whom you appear as lights in the world.

Philippians 2:15, NASB

Blessings on the family: "the righteous man leads a blameless life; blessed are his children after him" (Proverbs 20:7).

Blessings of life: "truthful lips endure forever, but a lying tongue lasts only a moment" (Proverbs 12:19).

Blessings of prosperity: "the house of the righteous contains great treasure, but the income of the wicked brings them trouble" (Proverbs 15:6).

God requires us to be honest and not dishonest. Let us examine ourselves and repent of any area where dishonesty has crept in – or even become a way of life for us. As we repent He will forgive and this will restore our fellowship with Him – and others.

Lord God, I don't want my relationship with you spoiled in any way. I cannot say I have never lied or been dishonest – forgive me for the times I have been dishonest, in words, deeds and thoughts. Your word says I need to put things right with those I have sinned against – as I do this help me bring forth your fruits of the Spirit – humility, honesty, faith and courage and above all love for my neighbours – when I reach out to them in confession and repentance and ask forgiveness. If I need to give restitution I ask for the grace to accomplish this with a willing loving heart. Thank you, Father, for your loving discipline that keeps us in your Kingdom ways and in your blessing. Amen

Work and our talents

If you work for 40 years you will work for approximately 70,000 hours, which is more than 10 per cent of the average life span. So whether you work from home, are employed or are in business, work occupies a significant part of your life. For most people, work provides the primary source of income, but for whom do you really work and how should you approach your work?

In Colossians 3:23-24 Paul tells us that, "whatever you do, do your work heartily, as for the Lord rather than for men.... It is the Lord Christ whom you serve" (NASB).

MATERIALISM

Probably the biggest deception regarding work in our society is the belief that a higher income can bring increased happiness and fulfilment. Many adults have jobs and are making adequate money, yet they are not fulfilled. Many say, without hesitation, that they pursued their career because it offered prestige and a route to a high income. They subsequently see the mistake of making decisions based primarily on income. Money does not provide satisfaction. As Paul wrote, "the love of money is a root of all kinds of evil" (1 Timothy 6:10). Note that Paul says that it is *a* root – not *the* root.

He who labours as he prays lifts his heart to God with his hands.

St Bernard of Clairvaux

God's work done in God's way will never lack God's supply.

Hudson Taylor

ATTITUDE

Work often comes with built-in reasons for dissatisfaction. It may be repetitive and boredom may ensue. Disillusionment may arise because of a lack of fulfilment, inadequate income, lack of personal development, the inability to advance, or any one of countless other frustrations. One of the primary purposes of work is not just to earn an income but also to develop character. While the carpenter is building the house, the house is building the carpenter. The carpenter's skill, diligence, manual dexterity, and judgement are being refined. A job is not merely a task designed to earn money; it is also intended to produce godly character in the life of the worker.

GOD'S PART IN WORK

Scripture reveals three responsibilities the Lord has in our work:

1. He gives us our abilities, "Every skilful person in whom the Lord has put skill and understanding to know how to perform all the work…shall perform" (Exodus 36:1, NASB).

2. He desires us to be successful as is shown in the life of Joseph, whose life was prospered by the Lord who "caused all that he did to prosper in his hand" (Genesis 39:2-3, NASB).

3. Knowing that we work "as unto the Lord", it is not surprising that God also seeks to direct our plans. In

Proverbs 3:5-6, we learn we are to put God first and "trust in the Lord with all your heart and lean not on your own understanding. In all your ways acknowledge Him and He will make your paths straight."

When love and skill work together, expect a masterpiece.

John Ruskin

Ultimately matters such as career development, promotion, and remuneration are not only about us and our desires, but also about seeking God's path for our work. Some leave God out of their work, believing that they alone are responsible for their abilities and successes.

OUR PART IN WORK

Scripture encourages hard work, "Whatever your hand finds to do, do it with all your might" (Ecclesiastes 9:10) while condemning laziness, "one who is slack in his work is brother to one who destroys" (Proverbs 18:9).

However, the Bible sets out a limit to the intensity of our work making it clear that we are not to work too hard. Exodus 34:21 instructs us that, "six days you shall labour, but on the seventh you shall rest." Rest can also be viewed as an issue of faith. Is God able to make our six days of work more productive than seven? Rest can also be a question of trust – trusting God to provide as we lead a balanced life that keeps Him as our first priority as well as maintaining time for Him and also our family.

In all toil there is profit, but mere talk tends only to want.

Proverbs 14:23, RSV

Our people must learn to devote themselves to doing what is good, in order that they may provide for daily necessities and not live unproductive lives.

Titus 3:14

OUR TALENTS GLORIFY GOD

It honours the Father when we are true to our Creator. We please God when we act the way we are designed to be. The workplace provides more than mere income for our provision and tithe; it is also a primary place for our witness. Ministry is not the work of full-time professionals; it is the work of full time followers of Christ – all of us. As 1 Corinthians 12:5 says, "There are varieties of ministries and the same Lord" (NKJV)

Thank you Lord for opportunities to work for You – not simply to earn money. Whatever I do, I choose to work for You – you are the best boss! You care about me, encourage me, discipline me, direct me, open doors for me at just the right time. You provide for me – help me to keep You before me as I work. To use the skills and talents you have planted in me personally to use them fully to extend your Kingdom, Thank you also that you don't expect me to work 24/7 but command me to rest one day a week. Thank you Lord! There always seems so much to do – I will not feel guilty for taking some time to rest – help me to find my rest in You – even as I work. Amen

Marriage and money

Money problems are a common cause or major contributory ingredient in marriage breakdown. My former Pastor, Johnny Hunt, says the two primary causes of marital breakup are money and lack of communication and the reason they are not communicating is because of money problems.

The exponential growth in secured and unsecured debt over the past fifty years has fed an increasingly materialistic society with a 'have it, and have it now' mentality – buying on credit, paying later or stretching the home loan. There is no age barrier to this debt-creep – even those who are retired are not as free of debt as they once might have envisaged.

The financial quagmire that many households face is exacerbated by investments that rise only to plummet and a 'retirement pot' that is often inadequate. Thus the seeds of anxiety and discord are never far from the front door. To make matters worse, it is quite possible that the handling of money did not receive more than a few brief mentions when you lived at home – and if *you* have children that may still be the case.

> *There is a powerful relationship between our true spiritual condition and our attitude and actions concerning money and possessions.*
>
> **Randy Alcorn**

> *The challenge for most people is that their earning capacity does not match their yearning capacity.*

You make deposits in your spouse's trust account by good communication, honesty, and transparency with money.

Howard Dayton

TRANSFORMING YOUR THINKING

Like a course of treatment, it is important that you stay aligned as the canvas of what the Bible has to say about your finances becomes your own masterpiece. When you married you made a covenant with one another and as you did so you became 'one flesh', so if you are reading this and your spouse is not, then lovingly encourage him/her to join with you in this study. The way forward is not found in simply implementing a financial plan, but in allowing the word of God to transform your thinking and your planning. Rediscover the joy of communicating about these matters with one another – and, if you have children, plan how you can help them because the challenges when they leave home may be greater than ever before.

The majority of warnings in Christ's messages were to the wealthy, not the poor.
Just having an abundance is not a sign of God's blessings. A disciplined lifestyle with an abundanc is greater witness than the abundance could ever be.

Larry Burkett, Co-Founder Crown Financial Ministries, 1939–2003

TAKING SOME PRACTICAL STEPS

Here are some steps that I hope will help –
they work for others, so why not you?

Step 1: Plan to do this together

Often one spouse takes responsibility for
the finances. I am an accountant and have
owned three businesses, yet my wife, who has
no bookkeeping qualifications, masterminds
our finances – pretty much from A to Z. A
word to the spouse who is stronger in this
area – do not dominate or get frustrated if
your partner is not as good at this as you
are. Do what you can to lovingly help your
partner understand the household's finances.

Step 2: Pray

I recommend you both get on your knees
and pray. It is not that God will not hear your
prayers if you do not, but rather you are giving
God the honour He deserves – as you bend your
knees you are submitting your will to Him
as you both draw close to Him, and so to one
another.

Step 3: Status

I strongly recommend that you each take
five minutes to write down what state you
think your finances are in – what needs fixing
and what does not. Alongside each statement
you might write a number from 1 (easy) to
5 (very difficult) to indicate how difficult a
situation it is to address. You might also wish
to add another column for the number of
months/years you think it will take to change
the situation. Then compare what you have
each written and prepare a combined status

*The effects of financial
bondage on a marriage
relationship are
measurable in the
statistics of failed
marriages. A marriage is
a partnership – much like
the right and left hands
of the same person. God's
Word says that two people
become one.*

Larry Burkett

*And if a Kingdom be
divided against itself, that
Kingdom cannot stand.
And if a house be divided
against itself, that house
will not be able to stand.*

Mark 3:24-25

I also tell you this: If two of you agree here on earth concerning anything you ask, my Father in heaven will do it for you.

Matthew 18:19, NLT

report to see where you are in agreement and where there are differences in how you see the situation – or perhaps where there might be some 'blind spots.' Throughout, make sure you remain positive and share together as humbly as you do when you pray.

Step 4: Pray again!
Find time for one another – enjoy each other's company.

I have watched over 100,000 families over my years of investment counselling.
I always saw greater prosperity and happiness among those families who tithed than among those who didn't.

Sir John Templeton, Investor and philanthropist, 1912–2008

In your word, Father, you reveal the relationship between your son Jesus and your Church as a marriage – Jesus the bridegroom and us His bride. You also show us Jesus loves us even to death on a cross. Help me to be like Jesus in my marriage. Help me to share openly the things that worry me – to listen to my spouse and hear their worries and concerns about our finances. Help us as we work together to get our financial habits under your control – to agree together – with You – and embark on Your 'treatment' for the health and wholeness of our finances and ultimately our marriage. Draw us together in a fresh new way to enjoy time with each other, free from the anxiety of money problems. Thank you that you love your bride and provide a way to financial freedom as we work together – You, my spouse and me, in your eternal triangle of love. Amen

DAY 29

Training our children – part 1

I have always been intrigued that the following verse (Proverbs 22:7) tells us that the borrower is slave to the lender. The message? Parents train your children how to handle their finances.

Mark Lloydbottom

A child who is allowed to be disrespectful to his parents will not have true respect for anyone.

Billy Graham

If you have children God has given you a tremendous opportunity and responsibility to nurture them and allow Him to use you to shape and mould them into all God desires for them.

Our materialistic, 'have it now' society impacts and influences each of us. Children today are affected by a range of external factors, including advertisements, the Internet, media stars, peers and so on. Whatever influences your children probably also influences their spending 'requests.'

I have heard so many parents tell me that they never spent time training their children how to handle money. Sometimes that was because the parents had money problems of their own. Children learn by example and although you might not feel you are qualified, you are – because you are the parents! Our children need training, shaping and moulding more than ever before – and not only in how to handle money.

NURTURING YOUR CHILDREN

Every child has his or her own God-given gifts and strengths, and it is a parent's responsibility to help the child identify these and encourage their development.

One of the ways we can help our children is to teach them how to be good stewards of the resources God provides. If this is done properly, God can use parents to leave a legacy of faith to our children.

How do we do it? How do we teach them to be good stewards?

The less I spent on myself and the more I gave to others, the fuller of happiness and blessing did my soul become.

Hudson Taylor,
Missionary, 1832 – 1905

LOVE

Share the love of Jesus and set an example by loving your spouse, family and others. In fact Paul tells us to, "Let him who boasts boast in the Lord" (1 Corinthians 1: 31). We should share the truth of God's love and ways whenever we can. We should be a constant source of love and encouragement for our children. Think of it as being your children's greatest fan. Yes, there is a time for discipline, but there is also a time for encouragement.

If our children know that we truly love them they will be more willing to let us lead them and speak truth into their lives. Look at 1 Corinthians 13: 4-6 for the characteristics of love and ask yourself if you are displaying this kind of love to your children. Do your children know they are more important than your job, your standard of living, your hobbies? Take time to show your love and invest in them.

A student is not above his teacher, but everyone who is fully trained will be like his teacher.

Luke 6:40

PROVIDE

Many of the financial decisions we make now will affect our children in the future, so we need to make sure our children's needs are factored into our decision-making. Possible areas for consideration include education,

Children imitate everything we do, whether important or unimportant, healthy or unhealthy. Sometimes our children will fail to listen to us. Rarely will they fail to imitate us.

Randy Alcorn

weddings and perhaps assistance with initial housing costs.

This does not mean that we should provide every pound for every activity our child does, rather that we need to have a plan in place to provide for their needs. You and your spouse may decide that you want to earn more money to help pay for some of their needs. Teaching them the value of work is important.

MODEL

When Paul was talking to the Church at Corinth and encouraging them to be more Christ-like, he said these words recorded in 1 Corinthians 11:1, "Follow my example, as I follow the example of Christ." Paul realised the importance of being a model, an example, of what he was teaching. The same thing

Parents cannot establish financial discipline in their children if they themselves are undisciplined. Teach your children that everyone needs to live on a budget. Children who have been taught the basic principles of money management early and have proved their ability to use them wisely could be trusted to handle a debit or credit card with no problem.

Larry Burkett, Co-Founder Crown Financial Ministries, 1939–2003

goes for our children. In most cases, what we do will have a greater impact than what we say. James Dobson wrote, "When children are young, they follow our advice, when they are older, they follow our example." Our instruction will not be effective if we do not model it.

> *I have chosen him, so that he will direct his children and his household after him to keep the way of the Lord by doing what is right and just.*
>
> **Genesis 18:19**

If your children followed your example today, what condition would they be in tomorrow? Would your example prepare them to be good stewards when they grow up, or would it cause them to make some of the mistakes you may have made?

Do not lose hope! Even if you have not started out right and modelled for your children the proper way to give, save and spend in a manner that honours God, you can always start today!

Thank you, Father God, for the wonderful gift of children – and the opportunity to love and teach them about You and how You want them to live. Forgive me, Father, where I have not been a good example to them – saying one thing and doing another. Help me to model moral and practical truth in every part of my life – and in so doing show them the life skills to live in financial freedom as I also continue to learn how to do so myself. Amen

DAY 30

Training our children – part 2

TRAINING OUR CHILDREN TO BE GOOD STEWARDS

When athletes train for the Olympic games they have an instructor to help them develop and oversee fitness, diet, technique, strength, focus and any necessary sport-specific requirements. The athletes benefit from that instruction as their skills are honed and their abilities sharpened with the aim of peaking at the Olympics.

We are to train our children so that as they grow they will not depart from the path we lay down. Our training is like the railway lines over which the train reaches its destination, time and time again. We teach them the paths so that they will unerringly follow. "He leads me in the paths of righteousness" (Psalm 23:3).

Fathers, do not exasperate your children; instead, bring them up in the training and instruction of the Lord.

Ephesians 6:4

TRAIN BUT DO NOT EXASPERATE

In those well-known verses in Ephesians 6:1-3, Paul instructs children to obey their parents. However, in verse 4 fathers are instructed not to exasperate their children. Our children learn discipline and respect by being instructed in the ways of the Lord. Trying to discipline and command respect from our children without bringing them up in the training and instruction of the Lord only exasperates them.

One of the areas that is extremely important to instruct children in is how to be good stewards of the resources that God gives them and will provide for them in the future. If children are not prepared, they will have a difficult time managing money and other resources. If we do not teach them, the likelihood is that marketers and advertisers will!

Children soak up parental attitudes and behavioural traits like a sponge soaks up water. Children have more need of good role models than of critics.

Mark Lloydbottom

Teach our children that God owns everything by allowing them to see this principle in your life. Pray about your material needs and let God provide them without borrowing so your children can see God is real.

Larry Burkett, Co-Founder Crown Financial Ministries, 1939-2003

RECOGNISE

In our society, children have a large amount of disposable income as well as a persuasive influence in a significant number of family purchases. In fact, children are a powerful group of consumers on whom marketing and advertising companies spend seemingly endless budgets trying to capture their money – many times what is captured is the child's heart.

Giving a child money to put into the Church offering does not produce a generous child. If you wish to bring up your children to give generously, you must train a child to tithe from any money he or she receives from family, friends or any income from work.

WHAT TO TEACH THEM

We must teach children what to value, including the importance of having a relationship with God. We should also teach them about having a balance between, family, work and ministry. Stewardship is also essential – the practical principles of giving, spending, saving, having a spending budget, and who owns everything.

We should teach them how to make good spending decisions. Children need to understand that, as they grow up, the chances are they will not have enough money to buy everything they want. You do your children a disservice if you do not teach them to wait. It is better to learn this in the safety of the family rather than in the prison of financial bondage. Purchasing something that has been planned for some time and savoured is a lesson they can draw on in adulthood. They must choose based on what is most important to them. You may teach them about budgeting for eating out and other forms of entertainment such as the cinema. For many families this is the highest cost in the family after all the 'essential' household costs have been accounted for – discuss an appropriate approach to optional expenditure.

Children suck the mother when they are young, and the father when they are old.

English proverb

TEACHING TOPICS

Teach the value of working hard and seeing work as a privilege and positive experience: "All hard work brings a profit, but mere talk leads only to poverty" (Proverbs 14:23). Make sure they know that money does not grow on trees.

Observing their parents, two children were heard to argue about where money came from. One thought it came from the cash machine while the other insisted it came from the supermarket cashier, who was always offering cash-back!

Teach them the value of saving and earning interest: "Go to the ant...consider its ways and be wise...it stores its provision in summer and gathers its food at harvest" (Proverbs 6:6-8). Watch how your children buy with money given to them as opposed to money they have earned. They are usually more responsible with the latter.

Teach them about taxes – how they are collected and how they are spent. They may not pay income tax yet, but they will almost certainly pay VAT.

Teach them about credit cards and loans. You could do this by loaning them money for something and charging them interest. You may wish to share with them about your own debt repayments at some stage.

Teach them the importance of tithing and giving. Teach them the appropriate way to receive gifts – with a thankful heart. Teach them about the importance of having goals and dreams.

If you wish to leave much wealth to your children, leave them in God's care. Do not leave them riches, but virtue and skill.

Saint John Chrysostom, AD 390

...do not forget the things your eyes have seen or let them slip from your heart as long as you live. Teach them [God's laws] to your children and to their children after them.

Deuteronomy 4:9

So many different influences over children these days – so much to teach them, Lord! Help me not to exasperate my children in my desire to teach them your ways. Teach me patience and grant me wisdom to use our everyday family situations to bring your word and model the practical way to be good stewards of money. Help me Lord not to 'spoil' my children by doing everything for them – even though it may be a bit messy at times as they are given their responsibilities to run with! Give me love and patience as they learn. Bless our children, Father, as they learn to become good stewards and bless us as parents with the joy of seeing them running freely on Your tracks. Amen

Where to invest – part 1

The world uses every marketing technique it can to persuade us to invest our money. Sometimes we are told that returns are not guaranteed or that values may go down as well as up. History shows this is precisely what happens!

Paul tells Timothy, "Command those who are rich in this present age not to be haughty, nor to trust in uncertain riches but in the living God, who gives us richly all things to enjoy. Let them do good, that they may be rich in good works, ready to give, willing to share, storing up for themselves a good foundation for the time to come, that they may lay hold of eternal life" (1 Timothy 6: 17-19, NKJV). Paul's charge to Timothy is to insist that those who read God's Word understand their position and trust only in God and not in money or what money can purchase.

We should always be ready to purchase only those things that will outlast us because then our foundation will support us when the going gets tough. Money is an eternal resource designed to help fulfil God's purpose for our life. Money is not to be loved, but we are to love people and use money to prove our love for both people and God.

Four things on earth are small, yet they are extremely wise: Ants are creatures of little strength, yet they store up their food in the summer.

Proverbs 30:24-25

There are two times in a man's life when he should not speculate; when he can't afford it, and when he can.

Mark Twain, American writer, 1835 – 1910

Losses from unwise investments seem even more common in the Christian community than outside it.

Randy Alcorn

Over the next two days let us look at five eternal investment funds that would help us please God:

1. GOD WOULD BE PLEASED IF WE INVEST IN HIS ETERNAL INVESTMENT FUND

In Matthew 6:19-20 we read, "Do not store up for yourselves treasures on earth, where moth and rust destroy, and where thieves break in and steal. But store up for yourselves treasures in heaven, where moth and rust do not destroy, and where thieves do not break in and steal." We invest in this fund when our hearts are aligned with God's heart. The next verse in Matthew 6:21 advances our understanding: "For where your treasure is, there your heart will be also." Paul's well-known instruction in 1 Timothy 6:10 tells us, "For the love of money is a root [only *a* root] of all kinds of evil, for which some have strayed from the faith in their greediness, and pierced themselves with many sorrows."

WHERE TO INVEST?

We express our worship of God partly by giving back to Him what is His. Proverbs 3:9 gives us a key when it tells us to, "Honour the Lord with your possessions, and with the firstfruits of all your increase" (NKJV). We should plan to give back to God regularly, proportionately and in undesignated ways (Leviticus 27:28).

2. GOD WOULD BE PLEASED IF WE WOULD INVEST IN HIS HONOUR INVESTMENT FUND

We should honour one another and God. Romans 12:10 says, "Be devoted to one another in brotherly love. Honour one another above yourselves."

HOW TO INVEST?

By using some of your money to support those in need and by developing fellowship and relationship. Romans 12:13 says, "Share with God's people who are in need. Practise hospitality." And Hebrews 10:24-25 encourages us, "let us consider how we may spur one another on toward love and good deeds. Let us not give up meeting together, as some are in the habit of doing, but let us encourage one another – and all the more as you see the Day approaching." The Psalmist in Psalm 133:1 reminds us, "How good and pleasant it is when brothers live together in unity."

3. GOD WOULD BE PLEASED IF YOU WOULD INVEST IN HIS GROWTH INVESTMENT FUND

God wants us to grow and draw closer to Him as co-workers with Jesus Christ.

2 Peter 3:18 says, "But grow in the grace and knowledge of our Lord and Saviour Jesus Christ. To him be the glory both now and forever. Amen." Paul in his letter to the Church at Ephesus says in Ephesians 4:14-15, "Then we will no longer be infants, tossed

> *Vision motivates a person to give up now for the future.*
>
> **Alan Gotthardt,
> Financial adviser**

back and forth by the waves, and blown here and there by every wind of teaching and by the cunning and craftiness of men in their deceitful scheming. Instead, speaking the truth in love, we will in all things grow up into him who is the Head, that is, Christ."

For where your treasure is, there your heart will be also.

Luke 12:34

HOW TO INVEST

Help myself and others grow in knowledge and wisdom. Proverbs 10:16 says, "The labour of the righteous leads to life, the wages of the wicked to sin." We are to use our money to enhance our own and other lives rather than waste it on sinful practices. We are to use our money to purchase an education, gain instruction and become wiser rather than just holding onto money and loving it. Proverbs 23:23 says, "Buy the truth, and do not sell it, also wisdom and instruction and understanding."

Tomorrow we will look at two more funds for our investing.

When I stand before the throne
Dressed in beauty not my own;
When I see Thee as Thou art,
Love Thee with un-sinning heart;
Then, Lord, shall I fully know –
Not till then – how much I owe.

**Robert Murray M'Cheyne,
Scottish minister, 1813-1843**

How wonderful are your ways, Lord God – when we take our eyes off ourselves, look up and out and invest our time and money in you and your Kingdom we are twice blessed! As we give here in this world we are blessed and also blessed in eternity with treasure laid up in heaven – and no one can steal it or devalue it! Help me, Father God, to always remember that what I have belongs to you and I am your steward – money and possessions are some of the tools you equip me with to do the work you call me to – and also build my character to be like Jesus – not to make me feel good about myself. You alone, Father God, invest in my life to bring about 'interest' – faithfulness, self control, patience, love, goodness, kindness, which brings peace and joy. I love and worship you – where would I be without you? Thank you for all you've invested in me – and from a heart full of thankfulness – I willingly invest myself and all I have back into the safest 'funds' – in You and Your hands – the capital and interest already belong to You, my Lord. Amen

Where to invest – part 2

Whatever good thing you do for Him, if done according to the Word, is laid up for you as treasure in chests and coffers, to be brought out to be rewarded before both men and angels, to your eternal comfort.

John Bunyan

Continuing on from yesterday, we look at making more Kingdom investments...

4. GOD WOULD BE PLEASED IF YOU INVEST IN HIS EQUITY SERVICE FUND

In 2 Corinthians 8: 3-4, Paul says, "they gave as much as they were able, and even beyond their ability. Entirely on their own, they urgently pleaded with us for the privilege of sharing in this service to the saints."

HOW TO INVEST?

By using some money to expand your ministry – ministry means meeting needs in Jesus' name. Read 2 Corinthians 8:7-9 and Acts 20:35. Proverbs 11:24 declares that, "One man gives freely, yet gains even more; another withholds unduly, but comes to poverty." This verse says that the world of the generous grows and grows while that of the stingy diminishes.

Jesus also told us to pay close attention to the poor. Proverbs 28:27 says, "He who gives to the poor will lack nothing, but he who closes his eyes to them receives many curses." While James in 2:15-17 says, "Suppose

There is a time for everything, and a season for every activity under heaven.

Ecclesiastes 3:1

a brother or sister is without clothes and daily food. If one of you says to him, "Go, I wish you well; keep warm and well fed," but does nothing about his physical needs, what good is it? In the same way, faith by itself, if it is not accompanied by action, is dead."

Giving is a giant lever positioned on the fulcrum of this world, allowing us to move mountains in the next world.
Because we give, eternity will be different
– for others and for us.

Randy Alcorn

5. GOD WOULD BE PLEASED IF YOU INVEST IN HIS GLOBAL INVESTMENT FUND

We are called to play our role in the Great Commission – and there are millions who have not yet heard the Gospel message. Isaiah 49:6 says, "It is too small a thing for you to be my servant to restore the tribes of Jacob and bring back those of Israel I have kept. I will also make you a light for the Gentiles, that you may bring my salvation to the ends of the earth."

Financial independence is merely the opportunity to put your eternal investments into a higher gear.

Alan Gotthardt,
Financial adviser

HOW TO INVEST?

By using some money to take the good news around the world. In Luke 16:9 we read, "use worldly wealth to gain friends

Give portions to seven, yes to eight, for you do not know what disaster may come upon the land.

Ecclesiastes 11:2

for yourselves, so that when it is gone, you will be welcomed into eternal dwellings." Therefore as you live life here on earth, always share the love of Jesus with those whoever you meet so that when you get to heaven one day those same people will come up to you and say, "thank you."

Scripture tells us to store up treasures in heaven and not here on earth because one day we will enter eternity and what we have here will be left behind. If you are storing up treasures here on earth, every day that you live you are moving further and further from your treasure because one day you will die and leave it all behind.

HOW CAN I AFFORD TO MAKE THESE INVESTMENTS?

God's investment economy always works. Luke 16:11 says, "Therefore if you have not been faithful in the use of worldly wealth who will entrust the true riches to you?" (NASB). In other words, you cannot afford *not* to invest in these funds. Philippians 4:19 says, "And my God will meet all your needs according to his glorious riches in Christ Jesus."

Remember that giving your money to these funds is God's way to finance His ministry to the nations, our neighbours, our family and ourselves. However, we should recognise that God does not just want our money. He could have chosen another way yet this is the way He chose to show He really wants *us* to be an essential component of His plans.

Prepare your work outside, get everything ready for you in the field; and after that build your house.

Proverbs 24:27, RSV

THE PRAYER OF AGUR:
PROVERBS 30:7-9

Two things I ask of you, O Lord;
Do not refuse me before I die:
Keep falsehood and lies far from me;
Give me neither poverty nor riches,
But give me only my daily bread.
Otherwise, I may have too much and disown
you and say,
"Who is the Lord?
Or I become poor and steal,
And so dishonour the name of my God."

Lord God, you are the Lord of all Creation and see everything - open my eyes to see from your perspective - not just my little 'world'. Not just my family and friends - there are needy souls everywhere on this earth - show me where I can be part of the answer by investing my time and money. To invest the riches of your message of salvation in Jesus, in those who have never heard of your love and salvation, that they too may know and love you and enjoy your investment in their lives. I may at times only have two small coins, at other times a barrel full but used in your economy it can grow and multiply. Grow my character, Lord, as I step up to the plate of obedience and generosity - I too pray Agur's prayer - that in all I do I never dishonour you or be a cause of dishonour to Your name. Thank you, Father, for setting your hope in me - lead me on further. Amen

And my God will meet all your needs according to his glorious riches in Christ Jesus.

Philippians 4:19

Perspective

DAY 33

Work – productivity and income

Hard work is a thrill and a joy when you are in the will of God.

Robert A Cook, Evangelist and broadcaster 1912 – 1991

The average UK citizen can expect to live approximately 29,200 days, or 80 years. Despite what many people believe, work was introduced for our benefit in the sinless environment of the Garden of Eden – it is not a result of the fall of man. "The Lord God placed the man in the Garden of Eden to tend and watch over it" (Genesis 2:15, NLT). The very first thing that God did with Adam was to put him to work. God is always at work and He has created us to work.

PRODUCTIVITY AND SUCCESS

Productivity can be viewed as how much you are able to achieve based upon what you set out to accomplish. It is making those things that you plan happen. Almost everything you have in life comes as a result of your plans and productivity. Some are born with monetary advantages, or benefit from windfalls or rewards over which they have little or no control; but these are not the primary ingredients that give rise to a successful life. Productivity and success are dependent on one another. Productivity without a sense of accomplishment and contribution will eventually seem unimportant. At the same time, success will never be fully attained unless it is the result of outworking a plan thus giving rise to a sense of accomplishment.

COMPONENTS OF PRODUCTIVITY AND SUCCESS

Recognise who you work for. Paul tells us in Colossians 3:23-24 that we work for the Lord, "Whatever you do, work at it with all your heart, as working for the Lord, not for men, since you know that you will receive an inheritance from the Lord as a reward. It is the Lord Christ you are serving."

Although Joseph worked in Potipher's household, Genesis 39:2-3 makes it clear that, "the Lord was with Joseph and he prospered, and he lived in the house of his Egyptian master. When his master saw that the Lord was with him and that the Lord gave him success in everything he did." Joseph wasn't ready for the palace until he had been through the trials at Potipher's house and prison.

GOD GIVES PROMOTION

You should recognise God's role in your promotion in the world, "No one from the east or the west or from the desert can exalt a man. But it is God who judges: He brings one down, he exalts another" (Psalm 75:6-7). This demonstrates the difference in the way Christians should think about work compared to the way the world thinks.

SHUN DISCOURAGEMENT AT WORK

When workplace discouragement arises, there is always the risk of losing energy and

And masters [employers], treat your slaves [employees] in the same way. Do not threaten them, since you know that he who is both their Master and yours is in heaven, and there is no favouritism with him.

Ephesians 6:9

A man can only do what he can do. But if he does that each day he can sleep at night and do it again the next day.

Albert Schweitzer

interest in productivity. Sometimes there is a sense of feeling lost or hopeless, or maybe even feeling worthless. Overcoming these feelings is sometimes easier said than done. Remember in Ephesians 2:10: "We are God's workmanship."

EMPLOYERS

If you are an employer you will desire to see your employees blessed and successful. Employers have responsibilities, including:

- To lead fairly (Colossians 4:1)
- To communicate well and clearly (Genesis 11:6)
- To pay a fair wage (Malachi 3:5; Deuteronomy 24:14-15)
- To pray for godly employees for they are a blessing (Genesis 30:27; Genesis 39:4-5)
- Absolute honesty (Daniel 6:4)

Whatever you do, do your work heartily as for the Lord rather than for men.... It is the Lord whom you serve"

Colossians 3:23-24, NASB

EMPLOYEES

If you are an employee your work responsibilities, include:

Faithfulness (Daniel 6:4)

- Being a person of prayer (Daniel 6:10)
- Honouring his/her employer (Daniel 6:21)
- Honouring fellow employees (Proverbs 30:10)
- Communicating faith (Daniel 6:26)

Our work for Christ can be a common ground to reach others with the message of salvation – see 1 Corinthians 9:22. Whatever a person is like, I try to find common ground with him so that he will let me share with him. Do you see your workplace as a mission field? We have the opportunity and should share the good news of our faith.

SHOULD WE BE AMBITIOUS?

The Bible does not condemn ambition per se – indeed, Paul was ambitious: "We make it our goal to please Him" (2 Corinthians 5:9) – but the Bible does condemn selfish ambition: "But if you have...selfish ambition in your heart, do not be arrogant and so lie against the truth. This wisdom is not that which comes down from above, but is earthly, natural, and demonic. For where...selfish ambition exists, there is disorder and every evil thing" (James 3:14-16, NASB).

I shovel money out, and God shovels it back...but God has a bigger shovel!

Industrialist
R G LeTourneau

Thus the Bible is not against ambition, just the wrong type of ambition. Our ambition should be to please Christ – to work hard and pursue excellence in our work so that we please Him.

Most of us struggle with too many things to do and too little time in which to do them. The good can become the enemy of the best. Once you have a clear vision of God's call on your life it becomes much easier to evaluate opportunities and say, 'No' to those who would distract you from what the Lord wants you to accomplish.

I have two close friends. One has only average ability but because he has been

Do not slander a servant to his master, or he will curse you, and you will pay for it.

Proverbs 30:10

single-minded in his focus has had an enormous impact. The other is much more capable but has scattered his energies pursuing numerous projects with limited success. Knowing your work calling is important because it is a key factor in your productivity and success.

Someone once said, *"Work as unto the Lord... the pay may or may not be great, but the retirement benefits are out of this world!"* This is true, and you will find an additional benefit – increased satisfaction from a job done to the best of your ability.

The purpose of any Christian in business is to glorify God, not just make a profit.
One key to being faithful to the Lord is making decisions on the basis of God's Word and not on circumstances, feelings, or what is acceptable to society.

Larry Burkett, Co-Founder, Crown Financial Ministries, 1939-2003

Thank you, Father God, that right from the moment you created mankind you knew what we would need something to occupy our mind and hands, soul and spirit – and because we are no longer slaves, but friends, you want us to enjoy times of rest and relaxation and times of fellowship with you, to get closer to you. Thank you for the ability to work and to enjoy my work and do everything I put my hand to with all my strength – because you are my 'boss'. When I feel the work is tough I can turn to you for encouragement and strength to persevere. Help me and continually remind me, Lord, to recognise my responsibilities when I am employed and also whenever I may be called to the responsibility of employing or managing others, to practise what I have learned here today so that with a healthy ambition to serve you heartily and faithfully, I may enjoy your blessing and be a blessing to those around me. Amen

DAY 34

Finances and preparing for retirement

Plan ahead - it wasn't raining when Noah built the ark.

Think back to an event that occurred ten years ago. Can you remember the day you left school or your first day at work? Are these events you can recall with ease? Events that are way in your past are often easy to recall. Time never stands still and planning ahead is a godly pursuit. As you go through childhood, adolescence, the teen years and into work, marriage, home and children, the end of working life draws ever closer. What will you need to live on when you no longer go to work? What income will you receive from your pension – and when?

Unless poverty is your preferred choice, saving for retirement is a necessity. Many do not save at all, and for those who do, it is probable that their investments will not generate the income they expect or require. How does your faith interplay with your planning for the future and how do you ensure that your planning is adequate?

DO NOT NEGLECT TO PLAN AHEAD

Retirement is the point you reach in life when you no longer receive remuneration for what you do. Retirement planning can dominate the thinking of Christians who have sizeable incomes, resulting in overkill in this area. The fear of having to do without in the future causes many to rob God's work of the very funds He has provided. This money is salted away into pension funds for twenty to forty years. God's Word does not prohibit but rather encourages saving for the future, including retirement. As the Bible reads in Proverbs 21:20, "In the house of the wise are stores of choice food and oil, but a foolish man devours all he has," but the example of the rich fool given by the Lord in Luke 12:16-20 should be a clear direction that God's balance is – 'When in doubt – give; don't hoard.'

Retirement may be an ending, a closing, but it is also a new beginning.

Catherine Pulsifer

IT ALL BELONGS TO HIM

Whatever the size of your retirement provision it is important to remember that it all belongs to Him. Be sensitive to the inner prompting of the Holy Spirit and avoid the temptation to think, 'it's mine and I couldn't live without it.' Some day you may feel led to give more of it away, or none of it, that is between you and God. None of us will miss that final appointment when we meet Him face to face and give an account of our stewardship.

Does that sound foolish? I know young missionary couples serving the Lord who have invested everything to reach

A little sleep, a little slumber, a little folding of the hands to rest and poverty will come on you like a bandit and scarcity like an armed man.

Proverbs 24:33-34

But at the age of fifty, they must retire from their regular service and work no longer.

Numbers 8:25

(Note - this is the only Bible reference to retirement)

A retirement is a terrible thing to waste.

out and pursue their part in fulfilling the Great Commission. Remember that God commended the widow for giving away her last two pennies. He may or may not call you to give everything, but it is my experience that if you ask Him and listen you will hear Him calling. What a privilege to make an investment into a 'retirement home' that will last forever!

Of all the daily topics we look at together this is perhaps the one to which an entire book could be devoted. Listen to a financial adviser and you will almost certainly hear that you do not have enough. Markets may plummet, interest and annuity rates may be historically low – all seemingly justification for salting more away. Maybe you are drawing down on your pension concerned as to how long the fund will last. It is when you look at areas of your life such as income in retirement that you should remember that the wealth you are looking at is based on man's economy – and that this does not work!

When stock markets fall people with stock market backed investments sense the loss of the value of their investments. This serves as a reminder of what we read in Proverbs 23:5, "Cast but a glance at riches, and they are gone, for they will surely sprout wings and fly off to the sky like an eagle." The portfolios of many are decimated when markets fall – and eventually they do fall! And many people approaching retirement find they are not worth what they thought and that their trust is perhaps not as fully in Him as they thought. Ecclesiastes 5:10 tells us clearly, "Whoever loves money never has

Retirement for Christians should mean freeing time to devote to serving others more fully without the necessity of getting paid for it. If Christian retirees have this motivation in mind while looking forward to retirement, then the Lord really will find us doing His work when He returns.

Larry Burkett, Co-Founder, Crown Financial Ministries, 1939-2003

money enough; whoever loves wealth is never satisfied with his income. This too is meaningless."

SILENCE ON THE GOLDEN YEARS?

If you search the Bible for an understanding of God's instruction for you in the 'retirement years' you will find nothing. Some choose to continue working to 'boost their income.' Of course, it is legitimate to plan for retirement, but beware of allowing the golf course or more leisure time to become your goal for retirement.

Retirement provides an opportunity to work as a volunteer. Make yourself available to God and there will never be a work shortage. We live in a lost and needy world. We are surrounded by people who are destined for hell. Plan your finances for retirement, but do not forget to ask God how He can use you and your retirement finances to further His Kingdom, after all it is only His Kingdom that lasts forever.

By wisdom a house is built, and through understanding it is established; through knowledge its rooms are filled with rare and beautiful treasures.

Proverbs 24:3-4

Father God, forgive me when I become worried at the thought of how I am going to live and what I am going to live on when I retire. You are teaching me to be a faithful and generous steward and you promise to supply my needs no matter my stage in life. It is not just the continuing of my walk with you – my faithful loving Father – whom or what shall I fear! As I think about the future, help me to be wise in the decisions I take to provide for the days ahead. My circumstances may change, but you never change – as I review my life I see your provision all along the way – how can I doubt you now and be afraid. You never 'retire' Lord, you always love and care for us, and in the same sense, neither do we 'retire' as citizens of Your Kingdom. There is always much to be done, please lead me to those places' where you can reveal yourself through me, to those in need.

Amen

DAY 35

Planning to leave an inheritance

Making a Will is not everyone's first choice activity – in fact it is reported that only one in seven adults has a Will. Do you have a Will and does it reflect your current intentions?

In that it sets out His plan for the heavens and the earth, the Bible is God's Will, his covenant of redemption through Jesus Christ, and his plan for our inheritance. Today we will look at inheritance and in study 36 we will look at 'leaving it all behind'.

The Old Testament has many stories of how wealth was handed down from one generation to the next. In Genesis 12: 7 God appeared to Abraham and promised his offspring the land of Canaan (Israel). Abraham left everything he owned to his eldest son Isaac. Solomon inherited great wealth from his father King David (1 Kings 9:4-7). He too prospered and when he died his wealth passed to his eldest son, Rehoboam.

We will all die. As Isaiah told King Hezekiah, "This is what the Lord says: Put your house in order, because you are going to die; you will not recover" (Isaiah 38:1). Unlike in the days of King Tutankhamen when they believed that wealth would be available in the afterlife, we know that "Naked I came from my mother's womb, and naked I will

> *It is my happiness that I have served Him who never fails to reward His servants to the full extent of His promise.*
>
> **John Calvin**

> *There is no advantage in being the richest man in the cemetery.*
>
> **Colonel Sanders**

You can't take it with you but you can send it on ahead.

depart" (Job 1:21). We also know that someone else will inherit what we leave behind, "I [Solomon] must leave it to the man who will come after me. And who knows whether he will be a wise man or a fool? Yet he will have control over all the fruit of my labour" (Ecclesiastes 2:18-19, NKJV).

WHO BENEFITS?

We can only decide *before* we die who receives our wealth *after* we die. Recognising that passing on their wealth intact might not be a wise imposition on their children, these days the very rich may establish a charitable foundation, while others may leave relatively little, and some leave nothing but debts!

It is normal for spousal Wills to provide for the transfer of the major wealth to the surviving spouse. Nevertheless Scripture gives instruction in a number of areas including our children and grandchildren.

Children: the Bible makes it clear that parents should leave an inheritance to their children. The Bible contains many examples of parents passing on an inheritance and Paul in 2 Corinthians 12:14 instructs us that, "children should not have to save up for their parents, but parents for their children." Again in 1 Timothy 5:8 Paul says that, "If anyone does not provide for his relatives, and especially for his immediate family, he has denied the faith and is worse than an unbeliever."

Death isn't your best opportunity to give, it's the end of your opportunity to give. God rewards acts of faith done while we're still living.

Randy Alcorn

Grandchildren: Proverbs tells us that "Children's children are a crown to the aged, and parents are the pride of their children" (Proverbs 17:6), and Proverbs 13:22 makes it clear that parents should leave an inheritance to their grandchildren.

INHERITANCES CAN SELF DESTRUCT

God issues a powerful warning: "An inheritance quickly gained at the beginning will not be blessed at the end" (Proverbs 20:21). This represents one of the biggest challenges for the affluent. As the baby-boomer generation passes, unprecedented wealth is cascading down the generations.

Fortunes can tend to self-destruct by destroying the lives of those who inherit them. There is sobering evidence that an inheritance can have a powerful and harmful effect on the recipient. Studies show that the expectation of an inheritance diminishes personal drive, motivation to work and life purpose. In addition, a reason to look forward to the death of a loved one can have a devastating spiritual impact on one's soul.

A good man leaves an inheritance for his children's children, but a sinner's wealth is stored up for the righteous.

Proverbs 13:22

Now all the earth is bright and glad
With the fresh morn;
But all my heart is cold, and dark and sad:
Sun of the soul, let me behold
Your dawn!
Come, Jesus, Lord!
O quickly come, according to Your word!

Christian Friedrich Richter,
German theologian, 1676 – 1711

FIVE KEYS TO ENSURING THAT AN INHERITANCE IS A BLESSING

1. Train your heirs: Help them to develop financial wisdom.

2. Design the wealth transfer to develop your heir's character: Consider specifying amounts for education, car purchase, home deposit, business start-up capital or for grandchildren.

3. Evaluate the impact on your heirs: What is the worst that could happen? Do what you can to make sure God's resources are not wasted. In Galatians 4:1-2 Paul instructs us to provide guardians and trustees for our minor children, "What I am saying is that as long as the heir is a child, he is no different from a slave, although he owns the whole estate. He is subject to guardians and trustees until the time set by his father." Decide how much to give your heirs.

4. Decide when to transfer: Should you transfer now, on the occasion of a future event, or on death?

5. In all your planning, remember that it is a special privilege and responsibility to select the next stewards of the assets entrusted to you.

Father God, as your word says, none of us knows when we will die, but even in death you are ahead of us and have shown us how to pass on what you have blessed us with in this life, to continue to be a good steward even after I am gone! Remind me Father to get out the Wills we made years ago and look at them again to see how they line up with Your wisdom. Give us wisdom as we plan and prepare to leave an inheritance for our children and grandchildren. Thank you for this reminder to get our financial affairs in order for future generations so that what you have blessed us with is not wasted – and that the only debt to pass on is the debt of love! Thank you again Lord for your knowledge, care and interest in every detail of my life – what a wonderful Father You are. Amen

DAY
36

Leaving it all behind

Many people allow their wealth to define who they are, but God looks on us all equally; and furthermore he knows our hearts and minds.

'Leaving it all behind' suggests that we look at where our wealth goes when we die. In Romans 12:2, Paul encourages us to be transformed by renewing our mind, and in 1 John 2:15-17 we are reminded not to "love the world or anything in the world.... For everything in the world – the cravings of sinful man, the lust of the eyes and the boasting of what he has and does – comes not from the Father but from the world. The world and its desires pass away, but the man who does the will of God lives forever."

LIVING LIFE WITH AN EYE ON THE AFTERLIFE

We have an opportunity to live life today knowing that eternity is our destiny tomorrow, as it surely is. 2 Peter 3: 8 reminds us that in God's calendar a thousand years are like but a day, so in God's scheme of things it is just two days since our Saviour rose from the grave.

Modernity promotes acquisitive and material habits. Look around you and ask what you have that would not have been in your household fifty years ago. Look at the car(s) in the garage that might not have been there, or the technology in the living room. There is an army of over a million people seeking to sell us products and services that 'we need' or 'because you're worth it.'

He who provides for this life but takes not care for eternity is wise for a moment but a fool forever.

John Tillotson,
Archbishop of
Canterbury, 1630 – 1694

The apostle Paul wrote in 1 Timothy 6:8, "But if we have food and clothing, we will be content with that," but for the most part our society operates on the assumption that possessions equal happiness and that more is always better. Could we renew our minds by leaving behind thoughts of acquiring more possessions, and perhaps forgoing some of the products and experiences that media messages seek to persuade us we need?

SEEKING THE KINGDOM OF GOD

Matthew encourages believers to, "seek first his Kingdom and all these things [the necessities of life] will be given to you as well." In a world that seeks to marginalise God, or even shut Him out, even believers can find themselves reaching out for what the world has to offer and that which society

My soul, rest happy in thy low estate,
Nor hope nor wish to be esteemed or great;
To take the imprint of the Will Divine,
Be that thy glory, and those riches thine.

Madame Jeanne-Marie Guyon, 1648-1717

Do not store up for yourselves treasures on earth, where moth and rust destroy, and where thieves break in and steal. But store up for yourselves treasures in heaven, where moth and rust do not destroy, and where thieves do not break in and steal. For where your treasure is, there your heart will be also.

Matthew 6:19-21

says is necessary. Many people acquire goods they do not really need with money they do not have and then find they have to 'pay for, enjoy and maintain' what they have acquired.

I have found that it is possible to embark on a journey – and I stress it is a journey I am still on – to distance myself from what I own and have saved and regard it dispassionately. When markets and interest rates go down I am secure in the knowledge that it is God in whom I trust, and my faith is in God's economy and the certainty of knowing that He is my Provider and Father who loves me. As I know that 'tomorrow' I will be in heaven, I know that all I have belongs to Him and embracing that knowledge serves to change my heart, my life, my all.

INVESTING IN THE EXTENDED FAMILY

Then, having followed His Word and left an inheritance for my children and grandchildren and special bequests for those who have been close to me, I wonder what should I do with the rest? I have received little by way of inheritance and have worked hard for what I have. I have looked after my children, who are all now adults and financially independent. I am helping my grandchildren, my Church, the poor and so on. During my life I have learned that I will leave it all behind and so I return once again to my plans.

When a man becomes rich, either God gains a partner or the man loses his soul.

DRAWING UP A WILL

In our last study we referred to the fact that many people do not have a Will. As a former professional adviser I can say that of the hundreds of people I have advised many came to me either with no Will at all or with one that no longer reflected their wishes. One day I looked in the mirror and remembered the advice I had given to my clients about keeping their Will up-to-date and decided it was time to update mine.

God is going to have to take some people to heaven feet first, because they keep trying to hold onto everything they have here on earth.

Nearly all the advisers on estate planning and Wills I know expect to see a Will drawn up that leaves the residue of the estate in equal portions to the remaining children. But I started to think about adding my godly understanding of how to leave it all behind, and as I turned to Luke 16:9 I read about an investment that seems to have a compelling return! As Jesus himself said, "I tell you, use worldly wealth to gain friends for yourselves [in heaven], so that when it is gone, you will be welcomed into eternal dwellings." And later (v13), "No servant can serve two masters. Either he will hate the one and love the other, or he will be devoted to the one and despise the other. You cannot serve both God and money."

Then rise my soul and soar away,
Above the thoughtless crowd;
Above the pleasures of the day,
And splendours of the proud;
Up where eternal beauties bloom,
And pleasures all divine;
Where wealth, that never can consume,
And endless glories shine.
Henry Moore, 1732 – 1802

Do not boast about tomorrow, for you do not know what a day may bring forth.

Proverbs 27:1

THE ESTATE RESIDUE

I realise that having looked after all others in my Will I now have an opportunity to return to my maker what belongs to Him. What could the resources that are locked up in Christians' savings accounts do if they were released today to advance the cause of the Kingdom? How much is really enough? Whatever you may think, there is an unprecedented cascade of wealth passing down from the baby boomer generation – and I encourage you to pray about giving more back to Him, for that surely is what we should do. What you choose not to give in life, why not give in death? You have worked hard for what you have; now let it continue to work hard to save those who follow you so they may hear the good news of salvation.

Father God, thank you for reminding me to find or write a Will! In these days when so many are shutting You out from their lives, I long to see needy souls brought into Your salvation and to enjoy being a child of your Kingdom. As I think and meditate on your word show me where to 'invest' back into your Kingdom – where Your people are 'stretching' for you and Your life and Spirit are flowing unhindered to reach the poor and lost. Thank you, Father, for my inheritance of life in You that I enjoy because someone was faithful with their inheritance 'yesterday.' Amen

"A good man leaves an inheritance
for his children's children,
but a sinner's wealth is stored up for
the righteous."

Proverbs 13:22

5

Just
do
it

You cannot escape the responsibility
of tomorrow by evading it today

You canot escape
the responsibility
of tomorrow by
evading it today

All eyes on eternity

Our time on earth is but a jot compared to our time in eternity.

What is eternity? Are you certain that when you die you will go to be with God in eternity? Do we really recognise how short our lives are? There are many millions who have already died and yet everyone who has ever lived is still alive, including Adam, Moses, Paul, and all those who have known Jesus as Saviour. Thank God that eternity is very, very, long!

The Scripture in Mark 8:36: "What good is it for a man to gain the whole world, yet forfeit his soul?" is a question full of insight, but also one that presents us with a challenge.

It draws us to a comparison between believers and the love of the world. We are warned that gaining treasures in this life can be only temporary while there is an inherent danger that the pursuit of wealth can also compromise and endanger our eternal perspective.

Our real worth is what will be ours in eternity.

To 'gain the world' requires a focus and work attitude that can distract us from our spiritual focus. Sadly, many people permit this to happen as they seek to have what is expected or even seemingly required in life. We live our lives by what the world dictates and forget that Jesus told us that the world and everything in it will pass away. Thus, the world and what it offers acts as a decoy to lead us towards loss rather than gain.

SETTING OUR SIGHTS

Setting our sights on eternity gives us hope and sustains our soul, bringing a certainty that there is life beyond the grave – a life that is sustained by God. In Colossians 3:2-4, Paul tells us to, "Set your minds on things above, not on earthly things. For you died, and your life is now hidden with Christ in God. When Christ, who is your life, appears, then you also will appear with Him in glory."

For what will it profit a man if he gains the whole world and loses his own soul?

Mark 8:36, NKJV

When the world my heart is rending
With its heaviest storm of care,
My glad thoughts to heaven ascending,
Find a refuge from despair.
Faith's bright vision shall sustain me
Till life's pilgrimage is past;
Fears may vex and troubles pain me,
I shall reach my home at last.

William Hiley Bathurst, 1796–1877

The Oxford dictionary defines eternity as, 'existing always and unchanging, something that is perpetual or everlasting'. Our hearts and minds should be focussed on living a life that has a godly and eternal understanding. God is the same yesterday, today and forever.

The greatest use of life is to spend it for something that will outlast it.

William James,
Psychologist,
1842 – 1910

Contrast that with the world in which we live. Famous people come and go – one day they are important the next they are but a memory. Economies change, sometimes up, sometimes shaken and down. In the last half of the twentieth century and the first part of the twenty-first materialism has been rampant and society has had much with which to occupy itself – from myriad entertainment options to must-have possessions. Sadly, this is where most people's eyes are focussed. Isaiah 55:8 tells us that, "my thoughts are not your thoughts, neither are your ways my ways, declares the Lord." Use your possessions, capabilities and energy knowing that your time here on earth is short. Resist putting off what God has called you to do, for none of us knows when we will draw our last breath.

So we fix our eyes not on what is seen, but on what is unseen. For what is seen is temporary, but what is unseen is eternal.

2 Corinthians 4:18

REWARDS IN ETERNITY

What we do with our life, time, money and possessions has an affect on our rewards and standing in eternity.

Only one life, 'twill soon be past;
Only what's done for Christ will last

C T Studd, missionary and Ashes cricketer,
1860–1931
(His name remains inscribed on the Ashes urn)

WE LEAVE IT ALL BEHIND

We come into this world with nothing and we leave with nothing, or as Job 1:21 puts it, "we are born naked and we leave naked." Nothing in this world goes with us as we enter eternity – but we can use what we have now as part of our preparation for eternity. We can focus and apply what the Bible teaches. In 1 Corinthians 6:19 Paul tells the Christians at Corinth that their, "bodies are a temple of the Holy Spirit, who is in you, whom you have received from God? You are not your own."

You'll not get to heaven and hear God say you should have given less.

EVERYTHING WILL BE DESTROYED

Earthly goods will not last forever – they are destined to be totally annihilated. "The day of the Lord will come like a thief. The heavens will disappear with a roar; the elements will be destroyed by fire, and the earth and everything in it will be laid bare. Since everything will be destroyed in this way, what kind of people ought you to be? You ought to live holy and godly lives" (2 Peter 3:10-11). Understanding the temporal nature of our possessions should influence us as we consider how we manage our money and possessions.

IMPACTING ETERNITY TODAY

What are the choices facing you now? How does an eternal perspective influence your decisions? Martin Luther said that on his calendar there were only two days: 'today' and 'that day.' Maybe we should invest all that we are and have only in *that* day.

The length of our days is seventy years or eighty, if we have the strength; yet their span is but trouble and sorrow, for they quickly pass, and we fly away.... Teach us to number our days aright, that we may gain a heart of wisdom.

Psalm 90:10-12

I praise you, Lord, for choosing to live with me through-out eternity and for allowing me to live with you. Thank You, Father God, that you want us in your presence and for giving us the way in, through Your Son Jesus. Thank you, Father, for the years you give us to be prepared for heaven and eternity with You. I want to maximise the years I have left here – my thinking renewed, my character a reflection of Jesus and my earthly possessions and money used to bless You and others. I am thankful for your material blessings here and now, but glad I cannot take them with me – I won't need them in Your presence for you have prepared a place for me. Until that wonderful day arrives I ask for strength, perseverance and wisdom to live for You, attain financial freedom and enjoy each day knowing the delight of Your love and care. Thank You that each day brings me nearer to being face to face with You, in Your very presence, my Father and my King – for eternity! Amen

Making it happen
- part 1

As you near the end of these studies, what do you feel you have learned about God's plan for you, your wellbeing, and your finances? Have you shared anything you have learned with others? What decisions have you taken? Have any of them fallen by the wayside already? Have you set aside some of what you have studied or planned because the actions called for were too much or maybe you felt not achievable?

GOD IS TOTALLY COMMITTED TO YOU

God sent his only Son to die for you. That was a pretty big step that required His total commitment. He has a plan and purpose for you that one day culminates in eternity, but, until our time on earth is through and we are called home, we live here as temporary citizens. If coming to know Christ was the only purpose of our salvation why did heaven not become our home when we accepted Jesus? The answer is that God's calling extends beyond our own well-being and relationship with Him as Lord and Father to include being his co-workers in sharing our faith and the news of the gospel with those who do not know him and are destined for the fiery furnace of hell.

The plans of the diligent lead to profit as surely as haste leads to poverty.

Proverbs 21:5

The plans of the righteous are just, but the advice of the wicked is deceitful.

Proverbs 12:5

I believe there are three things that most people think about every day – their health, their relationships and their finances. With so much of Scripture advising us on how to handle money, wealth and possessions is it not wonderful to know that God's perfect will for our lives is that He entrusts what belongs to Him to us?

DEVELOP YOUR PLANS

Many people have personal plans concerning what they desire to achieve or do differently in the future. Financial plans are often vague and sometimes unrealistic – and they do not always reflect a godly perspective. On the other hand, there are others who have no plans because they cannot be bothered.

We first learn about God's architecture for planning in Genesis, as God, who was of course there *before* the beginning, planned and created the heavens and earth step-by-step. We read in John 1:1 that the Word (Jesus) was there with God, and two verses on in verse 3 we read that, "Through him all things were made; without Him nothing was made that has been made." In Genesis 1:2 we see the presence and role of the Holy Spirit who, "was hovering over the waters." Thus, in the first two verses we find the work of the three persons of the holy trinity: God the Father planning, Jesus the Son creating and the Holy Spirit watching over the waters. This work of the godhead is repeated in the New Testament as Jesus came to earth to do the will of his Father and the Holy Spirit came after His ascension.

When it is obvious that the goals cannot be reached, don't adjust the goals, adjust the action steps.

Confucius, Chinese philosopher, 551 – 479 BC

TRUSTING GOD IN PLANNING

As Moses faced the Red Sea, he held out his rod, the waters parted and he led the people of Israel to safety. He had to trust God for the safety of a nation as he led them between two walls of water that were several hundred feet high. Noah built a boat according to specifications given to him by God – he followed them and his household was saved. As David confronted the Philistine giant Goliath he faced a seemingly impossible task, yet he conquered. Did Moses, Noah or David have their doubts about God's plan? We don't know, but we might wonder if Moses felt apprehensive as he took the first steps across the Red Sea bed or if Noah sometimes had self-doubt as others mocked him for building the ark. And we can only imagine what David was thinking after the stone left the sling!

God gave us his written Word. It is our Creator's handbook, a book full of God's plans. It is good to have a written plan. Just as fear can seem more real at night only to recede during the day, so worries about finances dissolve away as you write down the plans God has revealed to you.

> *Make plans by seeking advice; if you wage war, obtain guidance.*
>
> **Proverbs 20:18**

O ever in our cleansed breast,
Bid The Eternal Spirit rest;
And make our inner soul to be
A temple pure – worthy of Thee.

Reginald Heber,
Church of England Bishop, 1783–1826

We will look tomorrow at some further strategies, but for today be reminded that as you have studied Scripture you have read verses direct from God himself, "All Scripture is God-breathed and is useful for teaching, rebuking, correcting and training in righteousness" (2 Timothy 3:16).

Father God – thank you for your written Word – the more I read and study it, the more I see and understand about You – my loving wonderful heavenly Father. I see the plans you have for us, how to live to please You, and for our total well-being. You also show us who we are! Not always a comfortable feeling – but vital for our spiritual and temporal growth and renewing our thinking. Forgive me, Lord, when I squirm away from your word because of pride, lack of humility or just plain apathy. Thank You for not giving up on us as your children – in Your amazing wisdom you know we need your discipline for our response to be obedience and self control. According to your plan help us to use the wisdom we keep asking for, not just for head knowledge, but to make a difference to our lives – my life, and those around me. Thank you for all the thoughts, ideas, and challenges you have given as I have studied and prayed my way through this study – I do not want to waste your word – I want to turn it into wise practical action with Your help and encouragement.
Amen

Making it happen
– part 2

Yesterday we looked at the beginning of the biblical journey to being led by God – making decisions and being resolute, setting aside doubts and worries, and having an eternal perspective.

Addressing God's will for your finances starts with seeking His direction through Scripture, counsel and prayer. You are never alone; His Holy Spirit dwells within. That is not to say you will not encounter moments of weakness, times of worry, or anxiety. But remember how Job held onto his faith when it seemed that everything was against him?

For God so loved the world that he gave his one and only Son, that whoever believes in him shall not perish but have eternal life.

John 3:16

CHANGING OUR THINKING

First, ask God to lead you as you align your heart and plans with His will.

Second, keep a godly, not a worldly, mindset.

Now, write down where you feel you have been successful financially. Do not lose sight of what you have already achieved.

Then, write down everything you feel is a problem or in need of a change or decision. It is time to see this in front of you and confront the issues. Recognise that the word of God gives you the spiritual insight, wisdom and strength that you need. As you look at what

When your outgoings exceed your income, your upkeep will lead to your downfall.

Paul's Change of Plans:
*Now this is our boast:
Our conscience testifies
that we have conducted
ourselves in the world,
and especially in our
relations with you, in the
holiness and sincerity that
are from God. We have
done so not according
to worldly wisdom but
according to God's grace.*

2 Corinthians 1:12

*We can change, slowly
and steadily, if we set our
will to it.*

Robert H Benson,
Anglican minister,
1871 – 1914

*You should give according
to your income, lest
God make your income
according to your giving.*

you have written, keep praying that God
will continue to show you the way forward.
Remember that, "The one who is in you is
greater than the one who is in the world"
(1 John 4:4).

When you have everything in front of you,
try to prioritise your list. Maybe some of your
points are problems while others just need
decisions.

Then alongside each point you wish to
address note what you want to achieve. For
example, you may have written that your
expenditure is greater than your income, in
which case you could say that you would like
a balanced budget.

It is important to resist thinking that
simply doing this will automatically fix the
situation. While this could happen, it is likely
that you are addressing situations that have
existed for some time. So, unless you are
facing an emergency, such as impending
bankruptcy, allow yourself time and space
to work through these situations using the
godly insights and wisdom you have gained
from your studies. It may have taken time for
the items on your list to warrant the attention
they are now receiving. Do not pressurise
yourself now and squeeze out the opportunity
for God to continue to mould you as you trust
Him in these matters.

THE NEXT STEPS

Do not try to fix everything at the same
time. Look at your list and select two items.
Alongside each of these describe the steps you
could take in the next thirty days to advance or
improve the change you feel called to address.

If, for example, your spending is greater than your income you should start by recording *all* your income and expenditure over the next thirty days. You will find sample forms for printing or spreadsheets to use at Your Money Counts on **www.yourmoneycounts.org.uk**

> *For everyone who asks receives; he who seeks finds; and to him who knocks, the door will be opened.*
>
> **Matthew 7:8**

SHOULD YOU SEEK COUNSEL?

On day 16 we looked at what the Bible has to say about the wisdom of counsel. Do you know a godly person who could advise you? If not, ask those to whom you turn for spiritual guidance.

Finally, make sure that what you have decided to do is within your capability. It is better to succeed by taking small steps than to fail trying a giant leap. Then, as you begin to accomplish small successes, move on to the bigger hurdles.

Remember, our financial decisions are integral to who we are; they partly reflect us and our spirituality. Decide that this will be a godly walk and that you will start to achieve what you have purposed in your heart.

From strength to strength go on;
Wrestle, and fight, and pray,
Tread all the powers of darkness down,
And win the well fought day.

Charles Wesley, 1707–1788

Thank you, Father God, for your encouragement. I'm ready and willing Lord to go on this walk and trust You to help me achieve financial freedom. I will use these practical steps; they will really help me to see and 'earth' what I have been thinking through and not forget! Keep me totally honest and realistic as I capture my thoughts, write things down, plan and prioritise for action – I can see the way ahead more clearly. A step at a time – steadily. If I get impatient for the 'instant fix' – draw me back close to your side – be my Shepherd – tend me and lead me – to those quiet waters of financial freedom and the peace of heart and mind that it brings. My trust is in You; with Your guidance I will arrive there! Amen

Just stretching

How do you feel when you are asked to give? I do not mind sharing that I do not always find myself a cheerful giver. I am far from convinced that giving is a natural activity, even though there have been many occasions when I was really excited about making a gift or responding to an appeal. We have been saved from hell by the death of our Saviour who gave more than we will ever be asked to give. So, feast on the words of your Church leaders as they preach on stewardship for they act as a reminder for our hearts to be finely tuned to outwork stewardship.

God has given us two hands, one to receive and the other to give.

Billy Graham

TIME TO BUILD THE HOUSE

About 500 years before the birth of Christ, a group of people responded to trusting God in much the same way as some do today. Haggai tells us of a group of Jews who were released from captivity to return to Jerusalem to rebuild and restore the temple of God. The temple was a sacred place where the glory of God resided and without it there was no place to worship.

Although rebuilding the temple was a huge task, initially there was great enthusiasm. Before beginning the work, the people took the altar of God and restored it to

We make our plans, and then our plans turn around and make us.

F Boreham – Theologian

*Trust in the Lord forever,
for in God the Lord, we
have an everlasting rock.*

Isaiah 26:4

*Wherever you are in
your journey to a more
generous life, God wants
to take you further!*

its central place. Even though there were no walls or foundations for the temple, the altar was in place so they gathered to worship God.

After a while, however, the people's enthusiasm began to wane and the building work came to a halt, so God sent Haggai to get them back on schedule. Haggai preached a compelling sermon on their refusal to do what the Lord had told them to do: "This is what the Lord Almighty says: "These people say, 'The time has not yet come for the Lord's house to be built'" (Haggai 1:2). This was an excuse because they had spent the Lord's money on themselves and wanted to postpone the project. They did not have the time to do what the Lord wanted them to do!

Does that sound familiar today? Finding excuses and putting off the things we know we should do? Our trust and interest is in ourselves. God can wait...and wait. I find this true when it comes to obedience in tithing. Haggai had to give the people of God a strong exhortation by saying, "Is it time for you yourselves to dwell in your panelled houses, and this temple to lie in ruins?" (Haggai 1:4). Those people had time to build their own houses but not the house of God – and to make matters worse they were building upmarket houses for themselves!

GETTING COMMITTED

When you accepted Christ as Saviour you stretched out and committed your life to Him, starting on a Christian journey for the remainder of your days on earth before joining Him in eternity.

We all stretch and make commitments
– but then we have to take action on
that commitment. The 42,360 Jews who
were taken from Babylon to Jerusalem
were excited in the beginning and their
commitment was to rebuild and restore the
temple. I believe they really meant to do
just that. However, time and self-interest
intervened and they excused their lack of
action. They were willing to renege on their
commitment to God and depend on His
provisions while they took care of themselves.
Consequently the house of God lay in ruins.

*And do not be conformed
to this world, but be
transformed by the
renewing of your mind,
that you may prove
what is that good and
acceptable and perfect will
of God*

Romans 12:2

Many have given their lives to the Lord
and were initially excited and planned to
do all that God required of them. But time
and self intervened and soon self grew
larger than their commitment to God. Their
commitment to Him remains at a low level,
and perhaps the light of their commitment
is close to extinction. In Hebrews God said,
"Never will I leave you; never will I forsake
you" (Hebrews 13:5).

Are you just stretching now? Or did you
stretch in the past? Or have you given up on
something that God called you to do? If so,
do not feel condemned or think of yourself as
a failure, for God is longing for you to allow
Him to place His loving arms around you,
protect you and provide all your needs – just
so long as you will let Him. His love knows no
boundaries.

Father God, you are constantly stretching your hand towards me. I stretch towards you now and place my hand in yours. How foolish I am when I let my hand and heart slip casually from Yours – imperceptibly at first – but then I find myself in a desert place, looking back at a trail of unstarted and unfinished tasks behind me that you called me to complete. Thank you, Lord, that you do not condemn – forgive me, Lord, for my disobedience and selfish life. Show me again what you want me to build for you, for your Kingdom. Help me pick up my responsibilities again as a good and faithful steward. Thank you Father for your fresh reminders in this study – they are 'your rod and staff that comfort me' – keep spurring me on into being a good steward and move forward with fresh strength and purpose. Awake, my soul, and sing of Christ who died for thee, And hail Him as thy matchless King through all eternity. Amen

I end these studies with a verse that God gave Rhoda and I after we where baptised. May God bless you and keep you ever in Him.

"I waited patiently for the Lord, he turned to me and heard my cry. He lifted me out of the slimy pit, out of the mud and mire; he set my feet on a rock and gave me a firm place to stand" Psalm 40:1-2.